ABOUT THE AUTHOR

Neil Somerville is one of the leading writers in the West on Chinese horoscopes. He has been interested in Eastern forms of divination for many years and believes that much can be learnt from the ancient wisdom and practices of the East. His annual book, *Your Chinese Horoscope*, has built up an international following and he is also the author of *What's Your Chinese Love Sign?* (Thorsons, 2000). He has written for many magazines and newspapers.

Neil Somerville was born in the year of the Water Snake. His wife was born under the sign of the Monkey, his son is an Ox and daughter a Horse.

CHINESE SUCCESS SIGNS

Discover the Potential
of Your Chinese Sign

NEIL SOMERVILLE

Thorsons

Thorsons
An Imprint of HarperCollins*Publishers*
77–85 Fulham Palace Road
Hammersmith, London W6 8JB

The Thorsons website address is:
www.thorsons.com

Published by Thorsons 2001

10 9 8 7 6 5 4 3 2 1

© Neil Somerville 2001

Neil Somerville asserts the moral right to
be identified as the author of this work

A catalogue record for this book
is available from the British Library

ISBN 0 00 710683 1

Printed and bound in Great Britain by
Omnia Books Limited, Glasgow

In loving memory of my parents,
Don and Peggy Somerville

Knowing others is wisdom,
knowing yourself is enlightenment.
Lao-tzu

Contents

Introduction

Chinese astrology has been practised for many thousands of years, not only as a source of prediction but also as an indicator of personality. Each of the 12 Chinese signs has its own unique qualities and learning more about these can reveal where a person's best results are likely to come and where they may find the most happiness as well as the areas which require the greatest care.

Although there are many variations within each of the signs, which can be further examined by considering the element ruling the year of birth and the ascendant, or time of birth, it is remarkable how many people possess the main traits associated with their sign – how charming and yet resourceful Rats can be, for instance, and how efficient and orderly so many Roosters are. I know two born under the sign of the Monkey particularly well. One is straightforward and honourable but is most inquisitive and possesses a remarkably good memory, while the other Monkey is devious but at the same time so immensely likeable. These Monkeys are so different and yet both have important traits which are part of their sign. As you study *Chinese Success Signs* I am sure you will find this is the case with your own sign as well as with the signs of those you know.

How the Chinese signs began no one knows. One legend speaks of the Buddha inviting the animals of the kingdom to a New Year party. Only 12 turned up and in their honour the Buddha named a year after each, with those born in that year inheriting traits from the animal. The Rat, who never likes to miss anything, was the first to arrive, with the easy-going and sociable Pig being the last.

In some books the names of the Chinese signs are different, with the Rat being called the Mouse, the Ox the Buffalo or Bull, the Rabbit the Hare or Cat, the Goat the Sheep and the Pig the Boar. However, despite the name differences, the traits of the sign remain the same.

In order to find out your own Chinese sign, check the table of years that follows. The Chinese calendar is based on the lunar year and starts in late January or early February.

In this book I have used the masculine 'he' to refer to the signs, but unless otherwise stated, the term does cover both the male and female.

I hope that in *Chinese Success Signs* you will discover important features about your own sign that you will be able to use to your advantage. It is by being aware of your strengths and using them that your greatest success will come.

The Chinese Years

Rat	**18 February**	**1912**	**to**	**5 February**	**1913**
Ox	6 February	1913	to	25 January	1914
Tiger	26 January	1914	to	13 February	1915
Rabbit	14 February	1915	to	2 February	1916
Dragon	3 February	1916	to	22 January	1917
Snake	23 January	1917	to	10 February	1918
Horse	11 February	1918	to	31 January	1919
Goat	1 February	1919	to	19 February	1920
Monkey	20 February	1920	to	7 February	1921
Rooster	8 February	1921	to	27 January	1922
Dog	28 January	1922	to	15 February	1923
Pig	16 February	1923	to	4 February	1924
Rat	**5 February**	**1924**	**to**	**23 January**	**1925**
Ox	24 January	1925	to	12 February	1926
Tiger	13 February	1926	to	1 February	1927
Rabbit	2 February	1927	to	22 January	1928
Dragon	23 January	1928	to	9 February	1929
Snake	10 February	1929	to	29 January	1930
Horse	30 January	1930	to	16 February	1931

Goat	17 February	1931	to	5 February	1932
Monkey	6 February	1932	to	25 January	1933
Rooster	26 January	1933	to	13 February	1934
Dog	14 February	1934	to	3 February	1935
Pig	4 February	1935	to	23 January	1936
Rat	**24 January**	**1936**	**to**	**10 February**	**1937**
Ox	11 February	1937	to	30 January	1938
Tiger	31 January	1938	to	18 February	1939
Rabbit	19 February	1939	to	7 February	1940
Dragon	8 February	1940	to	26 January	1941
Snake	27 January	1941	to	14 February	1942
Horse	15 February	1942	to	4 February	1943
Goat	5 February	1943	to	24 January	1944
Monkey	25 January	1944	to	12 February	1945
Rooster	13 February	1945	to	1 February	1946
Dog	2 February	1946	to	21 January	1947
Pig	22 January	1947	to	9 February	1948
Rat	**10 February**	**1948**	**to**	**28 January**	**1949**
Ox	29 January	1949	to	16 February	1950
Tiger	17 February	1950	to	5 February	1951
Rabbit	6 February	1951	to	26 January	1952
Dragon	27 January	1952	to	13 February	1953
Snake	14 February	1953	to	2 February	1954
Horse	3 February	1954	to	23 January	1955
Goat	24 January	1955	to	11 February	1956
Monkey	12 February	1956	to	30 January	1957
Rooster	31 January	1957	to	17 February	1958
Dog	18 February	1958	to	7 February	1959
Pig	8 February	1959	to	27 January	1960
Rat	**28 January**	**1960**	**to**	**14 February**	**1961**

Ox	15 February	1961	to	4 February	1962
Tiger	5 February	1962	to	24 January	1963
Rabbit	25 January	1963	to	12 February	1964
Dragon	13 February	1964	to	1 February	1965
Snake	2 February	1965	to	20 January	1966
Horse	21 January	1966	to	8 February	1967
Goat	9 February	1967	to	29 January	1968
Monkey	30 January	1968	to	16 February	1969
Rooster	17 February	1969	to	5 February	1970
Dog	6 February	1970	to	26 January	1971
Pig	27 January	1971	to	14 February	1972
Rat	**15 February**	**1972**	**to**	**2 February**	**1973**
Ox	3 February	1973	to	22 January	1974
Tiger	23 January	1974	to	10 February	1975
Rabbit	11 February	1975	to	30 January	1976
Dragon	31 January	1976	to	17 February	1977
Snake	18 February	1977	to	6 February	1978
Horse	7 February	1978	to	27 January	1979
Goat	28 January	1979	to	15 February	1980
Monkey	16 February	1980	to	4 February	1981
Rooster	5 February	1981	to	24 January	1982
Dog	25 January	1982	to	12 February	1983
Pig	13 February	1983	to	1 February	1984
Rat	**2 February**	**1984**	**to**	**19 February**	**1985**
Ox	20 February	1985	to	8 February	1986
Tiger	9 February	1986	to	28 January	1987
Rabbit	29 January	1987	to	16 February	1988
Dragon	17 February	1988	to	5 February	1989
Snake	6 February	1989	to	26 January	1990
Horse	27 January	1990	to	14 February	1991

Goat	15 February	1991	to	3 February	1992
Monkey	4 February	1992	to	22 January	1993
Rooster	23 January	1993	to	9 February	1994
Dog	10 February	1994	to	30 January	1995
Pig	31 January	1995	to	18 February	1996
Rat	**19 February**	**1996**	**to**	**6 February**	**1997**
Ox	7 February	1997	to	27 January	1998
Tiger	28 January	1998	to	15 February	1999
Rabbit	16 February	1999	to	4 February	2000
Dragon	5 February	2000	to	23 January	2001
Snake	24 January	2001	to	11 February	2002
Horse	12 February	2002	to	31 January	2003
Goat	1 February	2003	to	21 January	2004
Monkey	22 January	2004	to	8 February	2005
Rooster	9 February	2005	to	28 January	2006
Dog	29 January	2006	to	17 February	2007
Pig	18 February	2007	to	6 February	2008

The
Rat

When it comes to charm, quick wits and resourcefulness, the Rat has few equals. And these qualities are shared by those born under the first of the Chinese signs.

Likeable and easy to get on with, the Rat uses his abilities to good effect. He is sociable, well informed and knows how to impress. He has a great deal in his favour and by using his skills wisely, he can make much of his life. However, in order to benefit from his strengths, he does need to be aware of some of his other traits, which, unless watched, can work against him.

On the positive side, the Rat is intelligent and quick-witted. Ever inquisitive, he likes to be aware of all that is going on around him. He is perceptive and shrewd and is particularly good at spotting opportunities. He is also resourceful and if he feels he can benefit from a situation, he is sure to try. Similarly, if his plans do not work out, he is usually able to extricate himself from the mess. The Rat is both cunning and a survivor.

Because of the Rat's abilities others often look to him for advice and they are rarely disappointed. The Rat does not hold back from expressing his true opinion and his advice is usually sound. Also, if criticism is due, he will deliver it. For an honest and unbiased opinion, the Rat is certainly worth consulting. He is also a good judge of character and this, together with his ability to relate so effectively, enables him to get many on his side as well as into his confidence. However, the Rat does sometimes act with an ulterior motive and is certainly not above using information he has obtained – or wheedled out of someone – for his own gain. He is, after all, an opportunist.

While the Rat may be good at getting information out of those around him, he is more circumspect about what he himself chooses to reveal. For all his *bonhomie* and friendliness, he likes to keep his own plans to himself. He is very much his own master and conceals his innermost thoughts and true feelings well.

The Rat is also ambitious. He likes the good life and recognizes that to get it he needs to apply himself and make the most of his abilities. Ever keen to get on and profit from the situations in which he finds himself, he is rarely still. He chases opportunities, engages in many different activities and is always keen to progress. He is very much geared up to action and throughout his working life, his tenacity and enterprise will lead him to some considerable successes.

However, despite this, the Rat can sometimes be his own worst enemy. His restless spirit is continually urging him forward and he does not always allow enough time to build on what he has achieved before moving on to other areas which he feels might offer a better return. Sometimes he will be right, but there will be times when more persistence would have brought him greater success.

The Rat also needs to feel stimulated and inspired by what he does. He likes to work with others and enjoys a challenge. If this is ever lacking and the Rat finds himself stifled or in too bureaucratic an environment, he can quickly turn from being a generally positive and upbeat person to someone who is critical, fussy and a stickler for the rulebook! A bored, discontented Rat is indeed a sorry sight, especially when he knows he is capable of so much. It is for this reason that any Rat who recognizes that he is in such a situation should lift himself out of it and seek new challenges. The Rat is, after all, intelligent *and* highly resourceful and he has it within him to make much of his life. As Benjamin Disraeli, himself a Rat, once declared, 'Life is too short to be little.'

The Rat is shrewd and has a good head for figures. He can enjoy success in financial matters and appreciates money not only for the pleasures and comforts it can bring but also for the security it can offer. Pleasure, comfort and security are all important to the Rat. Once he has money, he likes to keep tabs on it, so much so that to some he may appear thrifty and mean. However, this reputation is misplaced. To his family and close friends the Rat can be most generous and he will delight in giving gifts and spending money on his loved ones. Also, when it comes to himself the Rat can be quite indulgent, finding it hard to resist any treats that he may fancy. He may well save carefully for some time, only to splash out on some lavish spree.

The Rat is also a hoarder. He hates throwing things away in case they might have a use later. He will either recycle and re-use – and here the Rat can be very ingenious – or store items in a cubbyhole or shed. On the surface, the Rat's home may appear tidy and orderly, but the amount that he has managed to squirrel away will be a revelation.

The Rat's home is indeed important to him. It not only provides him with a secure base, but is also likely to be fitted with many comforts and appliances to help him live well. The Rat is a good homemaker and his eye for décor, quality and comfort is appreciated by his loved ones.

The Rat does like to be in control of his domain and will be the chief instigator of much that goes on there. He will, however, take a keen and fond interest in the activities of those around him. The family unit is important to him and he is both attentive and loyal to his loved ones. He makes a point of remembering birthdays, anniversaries and other personal events and his 'personal touch' is appreciated by so many. The Rat *is* thoughtful and he does care.

However, while he will always play an active part in the running of his home, the Rat does expect others to do their share. He will not tolerate those who may be tempted to sit back while others do all the work. No, in the Rat household, duties are spread evenly. The Rat also likes his home to be run in an orderly way and will not take kindly to bickering or arguments between family members. The Rat is all for a genial and stable atmosphere.

The Rat often has a large family and makes an attentive parent. Children will respond well to his imagination, wide interests and agreeable manner, and will often thrive under his care. The Rat keeps good discipline but at the same time encourages fun and allows his children sufficient freedom to discover their own individual strengths. He himself tends to leave his parental home early, but he will always try to maintain close links with his parents. Family connections are an important bond for the Rat.

The Rat also values his social life. He enjoys going out and meeting others and will invariably have a wide range of friends and acquaintances, often from many different walks of life. He also enjoys inviting them round to his home, either for a meal or chat, and makes a good host.

In addition to devoting much time to his home life and often active social life, the Rat keeps himself busy with a wide range of interests. He is a keen traveller and can be attracted to places that are in some way unusual and not necessarily on the tourist map. Being both creative and imaginative, he enjoys literature (and often writes himself) as well as music, theatre and the cinema. He is also practical and can enjoy handicrafts as well as carrying out projects on his home. The Rat has fine taste and does like the good things in life.

Both the male and female Rat take pride in their appearance, often choosing to wear smart, stylish and good-quality clothes. The Rat knows how to make the most of his often striking looks.

The male Rat certainly has panache. Well mannered, presentable and with wide interests, he makes agreeable company and possesses a ready wit. He uses his talents to good effect, having many friends and the ability to build up useful contacts. He is also keenly aware of his responsibilities, works hard and will always be eager to make the most of the situations in which he finds himself. But he can be prone to anxiety (which he conceals well) should things not go his way or whenever he has a difficult decision to take. He sets high expectations, but his wits, resourcefulness and canny nature will enable him to achieve much in life.

The female Rat also has an outgoing and breezy disposition. Easy to get on with, she understands others and will have a great many friends and contacts. She also speaks well and, with her charm, wit and keen intellect, has a knack of bringing others round to her viewpoint. She knows how to charm and uses her persuasive qualities to good effect. She is also creative and possesses a good imagination, although her desire for security and stability sometimes holds her back from actively pursuing her ideas. Her family are her first love and in addition to being an attentive mother, she is a fine and resourceful housekeeper.

Rats born in the summer and when supplies are plentiful are considered to lead easier lives than those born in the winter and the Rat will also have more luck if born at night. However, all Rats have the ability to make their mark in so much of what they do. The Rat has a keen and willing spirit and likes to be active, to be involved and to make the most of himself. He does indeed possess qualities that can lead him to considerable success. As William Shakespeare, himself a Rat, wrote, 'One man in his time plays many parts.' The enterprising Rat is capable of playing a great many parts through his often interesting and varied life.

SUCCESS AND WORK

The Rat likes to take the lead in all that he does and with his sharp mind and personable nature, he can certainly go far. He is also capable of original thought and is creative and imaginative. He is an opportunist and his resourcefulness, as well as survival instincts, will serve him well throughout his working life. So, too, will his superb ability to empathize with others and build up useful contacts. When it comes to winning friends and influencing people, the Rat is in a league of his own.

To really succeed in his work, though, the Rat needs both direction and stimulation. Then there is no stopping him, but he can get involved in too many activities all at once and dilute his energies and productivity as a result. If he can discipline himself and concentrate on given objectives, then he really can impress, but for many Rats, this is a lesson they will learn the hard way. The Rat finds it hard to resist opportunities, even if persistence in his present role would yield more in the longer term.

Another point the Rat needs to watch is that in his desire to progress, he can sometimes resort to tactics that might endanger his position. He likes living by his wits, but trying too hard and using devious means can backfire.

The Rat is, though, an effective communicator and has keen powers of observation. These talents have led many Rats to careers in the media. The Rat also excels when meeting and working with others and, where commerce is concerned, can make an excellent salesman and negotiator. The Chinese have a proverb which states, 'A man without a smiling face must not open shop.' The Rat is a good smiler.

The Rat can also make an effective politician, particularly as he is adept at winning others round to his point of view and using his skills and convincing manner to good effect. With his analytical mind, he can also find success in the financial and legal sectors, especially as both professions can often be so stimulating and challenging. He has a head for figures and can make a good accountant or banker. His resourcefulness also makes him an effective problem-solver.

Another area which attracts the Rat is show business, particularly as he presents himself so well and it will allow him to draw on his creative skills as well as be in the spotlight, something he invariably enjoys. Whether as a singer, musician, comedian or impresario, the Rat has the personality, skills and ability to make his mark.

The Rat can also be an inspirational teacher, particularly as he relates so well to others.

Generally, in his work the Rat prefers to use his mind rather than be involved in more manual tasks. He also enjoys challenges and seeing the results of his actions. Should he ever find himself in a position which stifles creativity and initiative, he will soon become restless and unhappy.

The Rat is also good at generating ideas but does tend to hold back when furthering them, even though he may not be averse to trying others' ideas or pursuing opportunities that he sees. In some cases, he should have more confidence and faith in himself. As has so often been said, success comes from within and by being prepared to follow through his own ideas, the Rat can achieve some particularly rewarding personal successes.

Another factor that sometimes can hold the Rat back is his fear of failure. He does so like to be considered a success and a loss of face will sometimes hurt him deeply. However, here again, he should remember that in avoiding taking risks – and occasionally failing in the process – he is denying himself the chance to progress.

However, provided the Rat uses his energies wisely and has faith in himself and his abilities, then he has it within him to go far and achieve considerable success in his chosen profession.

SUCCESS AND MONEY

There is no doubting the Rat's earning ability. Resourceful, adept at spotting opportunities and possessing a keen mind, he is capable of earning a good income. He also appreciates the value of money, which enables him to enjoy the finer things in life and provides the security he craves.

The Rat is astute in money matters. He will often sense a sound investment, seek out a good buy and ensure that money he deposits or lends generates a good return. He can be thrifty, only spending when he has to and making sure that he gets the best value he can. However, while he may go through spells of watching his spending, the Rat is indulgent and acquisitive and finds it hard to resist anything he fancies. Many a time he will save hard then go on a lavish spending spree. In addition to spending on himself, the Rat can be especially generous to his partner and close family.

For the Rat to make the most of his money, he should aim to set his finances on a proper and regulated basis, ideally maintaining a set of accounts. This way he will be better able to keep track of his income as well as be more aware of his level of spending. Also, he could find it helpful to set money aside for specific purposes so that it is less likely to be spent in some reckless moment. It could be to his advantage to set up a regular savings account – or even several accounts, each for a different purpose.

The Rat very much lives for the moment and does not always give as much thought to his future as he should. However, when he is able, he could find it in his interests to take advantage of tax incentives and save for the longer term. Over the years what he is able to put by can grow into an asset that he will be grateful for.

Should the Rat ever suffer financial misfortune, he certainly has the resourcefulness to restore his fortunes and, in some cases, better them. He is also versatile enough to put some of his talents, interests and hobbies to profitable use and can quite often earn money through freelance work or a second job. Again, his enterprise and creativity can serve him well.

Generally, in money matters, the Rat is shrewd and astute, even if indulgent!

SUCCESS AND LOVE

Passionate, attentive and with such an agreeable nature, the Rat will rarely be without admirers. And he loves being in love. He is a romantic, generous to those he loves, affectionate and interesting to be with. However, for any romance to succeed, there has to be trust and understanding on both sides and here problems can occur. The Rat often holds back from expressing his true feelings and to some, in spite of his outward charm, he can appear distant and aloof and so undermine what could have been a promising romance. The Rat himself will sometimes feel misunderstood and this again can stem from his hesitancy in expressing his feelings. Also, at the start of any romance the Rat, with his perceptive nature, will be keenly aware of the responses of the other person and by analysing every nuance, word and gesture, he may not give the relationship the chance it needs to become more established. He needs to be more relaxed, just let romance take its own course – and enjoy it.

The Rat may experience much anxiety and heartache as he searches for the right person to share his life. True, he may have a wide social circle and many admirers – in his early adult years he often has a flirtatious streak – but finding Mr or Ms Right is much more complex. The love of another is very important to the Rat and he will be looking for a partner he believes to be loyal, one who is prepared to let him be himself and is likely to value a secure and stable home life. In return, that person will be assured of the Rat's love and attentiveness as well as an often eventful life. After all, with the Rat's many interests and capers, there will nearly always be something of interest going on in a Rat household!

SUCCESS WITH OTHERS

The Rat likes people and because he is so warm and friendly, others respond well to him. He has charm, wit and style and is invariably well informed. He certainly makes agreeable company, but there will be some signs that he can relate to better than others.

With another Rat

With so much in common and so much to share, two Rats can get on well.

In the parent–child relationship, there will be a strong bond, with the Rat parent doing much to guide and encourage the young Rat. In return, the Rat child will thrive in the close, loving and protective atmosphere of a Rat home.

As colleagues, two Rats can make an effective combination. They have ideas, talent and ambition, and by working together towards a specific goal, can achieve a good level of success. But they must be careful not to overreach themselves and let their greed and competitive instincts undermine what they are setting out to do.

In love, two Rats are well matched. Loving, supportive and understanding each other so well, they will share many interests and pour much energy into their home, as both seek a secure and settled domestic life. If they have children, they will make attentive parents. Two Rats can make a close and devoted couple.

With an Ox

Although different in so many respects, the Rat admires the solid and dependable Ox and relations between the two signs will often be mutually beneficial.

In the parent–child relationship, the young Ox will respond well to the attentive Rat parent, valuing his guidance as well as becoming more outgoing as a result of his parent's sociable manner. There will be a good bond between them.

As colleagues, there will also be great trust, with each valuing the other's strengths. The Rat will appreciate the Ox's sense of purpose and determination as well as the way he brings order to so much of what he does. Both are hard and ambitious workers and together they make an effective team.

In love, the Rat will find strength in the Ox's quiet and confident manner. The Ox will be a steadying influence and help the Rat to channel his energies wisely. Both seek stability and security in their lives and with these similar values will enjoy a close understanding. The Rat and Ox are well suited and can find happiness together.

With a Tiger

Lively, sociable and enterprising, the two signs have much in common and relations between them can be good.

In the parent–child relationship, the Rat parent will do much to encourage the Tiger child's imagination and inventiveness, although he could sometimes find the young Tiger's independent-minded ways a trial.

As colleagues, both are full of ideas, enterprise and enthusiasm. When set on a common objective, there could be no stopping them!

In love, the Rat and Tiger will give their all. Both are passionate and outgoing and they will have many interests they can share, including a love of travel. However, both can be restless and strong-minded and they tend to have different attitudes towards money. If they can work at overcoming these problem areas, then with goodwill theirs can be an interesting and rewarding match.

With a Rabbit

Although the Rat and Rabbit are sociable and enjoy conversation, they do not always feel at ease in each other's company. Relations between them will be tricky.

In the parent–child relationship, the Rat parent's tendency to be frank and forthright can easily upset the young Rabbit's sensitive nature. With tact and understanding, the pair can, though, establish a satisfactory rapport as well as share many interests.

As colleagues, each can gain from the other, with the Rat particularly valuing the Rabbit's commercial acumen and fine organizational skills. However, their temperaments are different and a certain trust and camaraderie may be lacking.

In love, there is often very strong physical attraction. Sociable, home-loving and with interests they can share, these two can find their relationship starting with much promise. The Rat will particularly value the Rabbit's calm and discreet manner, but the Rabbit's sensitive nature as well as desire for a less active lifestyle can lead to problems. Both will need to make considerable adjustments if they are to build a lasting relationship.

⚮ With a Dragon

The Rat has a great admiration for the lively and enterprising Dragon and the two signs get on very well indeed.

In the parent–child relationship, the Rat parent will delight in the young Dragon's keen and inquisitive nature, and being such an effective teacher, he will enable the Dragon child to learn a great deal. There will be great understanding and much love between them.

As colleagues, these two will have ideas aplenty. Both are ambitious and enterprising and possess good business skills. The Rat will draw strength from the Dragon's enthusiasm and robust approach. Together they can achieve considerable success.

In love, what a match. There is a strong attraction between them and so much they can share. Sociable, outgoing and yet valuing their home life, these two will be supportive of each other. The Rat will feel particularly reassured by having such a confident, loving and respectful partner. Together they will find much happiness.

⚮ With a Snake

The Rat is intrigued by the quiet and reflective Snake and while their temperaments may be very different, there is a warmth and respect between them.

In the parent–child relationship, the sometimes shy and reserved Snake will learn much from an attentive and more outgoing Rat parent. There will be a strong bond between them.

As colleagues, these two complement each other well. Both are astute in business matters and they will combine their different strengths to good effect. The Rat will benefit from the Snake's more considered approach as well as his ability to plan ahead.

In love, the Rat and Snake are well suited. The Rat will become more settled and feel secure with a wise and reflective Snake as a partner. They both value their home life and are equally keen to make the best of their resources and combined skills. The Rat may sometimes need to goad the Snake into becoming more outgoing and stir him into action, but their love and respect for each other are invariably strong and both can benefit from the relationship.

⌒ With a Horse

The Rat may, for a time, enjoy the Horse's lively and spirited nature, but both can be forthright and sooner or later differences are certain to arise and sparks will fly!

In the parent–child relationship, the Rat parent may have difficulty in coming to terms with the Horse child's independent and self-willed ways. Both mean well, but their different outlooks will create problems between them.

As colleagues, both are ambitious, but each will want to take the lead. The Rat will view the Horse as impatient and impulsive and agreement between them could be difficult. Despite their fine individual strengths, they do not work well together.

In love, the Rat may fall for the Horse's lively and sociable nature and for a time the two could have a great deal of fun together. But the Horse is independent-minded, strong-willed and volatile, and the Rat may find this unnerving, particularly as he values security and a settled existence. If this relationship is to work, both will need to temper their forthright and critical natures. This can be a difficult match.

With a Goat

The Rat may enjoy the Goat's company for a time, especially as they both have a fondness for the good things in life, but their different attitudes will eventually cause problems between them.

In the parent–child relationship, the Goat child will value the warmth and protective atmosphere so often found in the Rat's home, but his easy and carefree manner will sometimes concern the Rat. They will love each other dearly, but relations between them may not always be the smoothest.

As colleagues, their different attitudes will again cause difficulties. The Rat will often feel that the Goat is too casual in approach and does not match his drive and ambition. With such a lack of understanding and rapport, the outlook is not good.

In love, the Rat and Goat may for a time enjoy each other's company. Both like the finer things in life, are sociable and have a good sense of fun. But the Rat may despair of the Goat's laid-back manner, his capriciousness and tendency to spend rather too freely. And once the Rat speaks out, his critical manner will cut into the sensitive Goat. Theirs will be a difficult match and will need much care, consideration and adjustment if it is to endure.

With a Monkey

The Rat has a great admiration for the vivacious and quick-witted Monkey and relations between the two signs are good.

In the parent–child relationship, the Rat parent will delight in the Monkey child's resourceful nature and ability to learn. He will encourage the young Monkey and guide him well. There will be good respect and a firm bond between them.

As colleagues, both the Rat and Monkey possess a keen and enterprising spirit and desire to make the most of their abilities. Each will encourage the other and together they could be on course for considerable success, provided they do not over-reach themselves or push their luck or sometimes greedy natures too far.

In love, the Rat and Monkey are well matched. They both have a wide range of interests and, with often similar outlooks, enjoy a good rapport. They are both great pleasure-seekers and will aim to live in style and comfort. Given their abilities and resourcefulness, they will usually succeed admirably. The Rat will feel reassured by having such a positive, lively and under-standing partner.

With a Rooster

Both may be sociable and outgoing, but both are noted for their candour, so peace is not likely to prevail for long.

In the parent–child relationship, the Rooster child, with his strong will and independent mind, will inevitably clash with his equally determined Rat parent! They will try hard and they will love each other, but relations between them *will* need care.

As colleagues, their different attitudes will clash. The Rat is all for making the most of the moment while the Rooster is an assiduous planner. The Rat will feel held back – and will tell the Rooster so!

In love, both are deeply devoted to their home life and there will be many interests they can share, but each likes to have his own way and again their blunt forthright natures will often clash. The more thrifty Rat may also be alarmed by the sometimes spendthrift tendencies of the Rooster. A turbulent and testing match.

With a Dog

The Rat and Dog may have differences in their outlook, but there will be much respect and admiration between them.

In the parent–child relationship, the Dog child will value the Rat parent's love and attentiveness and will aim to please. Admittedly, the young Dog may sometimes despair of his Rat parent's restless nature and constant desire for action, but he will learn much from him and there will be considerable affection between them.

As colleagues, the Rat and Dog will not find relations so easy. The Rat is always keen to make the most of opportunities, while the Dog prefers a more disciplined and considered approach. The Rat will find the Dog an inhibiting influence and their differences in outlook will undermine the work they do together.

In love, theirs can be a beneficial match. Both the Rat and Dog are romantic and passionate and attach great importance to their home life. The Rat will particularly value the Dog's loyal and dependable nature – and the Rat so likes to feel secure. Together they can find much contentment.

With a Pig

The Rat has a great respect for the genial Pig and with much in common, the two signs get on well.

In the parent–child relationship, the Pig child will thrive under the Rat parent's guidance and will learn a great deal. With interests they can share and enjoy, there will be a good bond and much love between them.

As colleagues, the Rat and Pig get on well and with their ideas, enterprise and abilities to seek out opportunities, they could enjoy considerable success. Both are ambitious and keen to make the most of themselves and each will be supportive of the other. Between them they have considerable commercial flair and the drive to make things happen.

In love, the Rat and Pig are well suited. Both enjoy the good things in life, are sociable and value their home life dearly. The Rat will benefit from having such a supportive, loving and good-natured partner. A successful match.

SUCCESS THROUGH LIFE

With his keen and outgoing personality, the Rat will invariably have a full and interesting life. There will of course be more difficult phases, but the Rat is resourceful and resilient and as he learns from his experiences, he will find his life generally becoming more rewarding.

The Rat's formative years will generally go well. With his inquisitive nature, he will delight in learning, in experimenting and often in taking part in imaginative games. He is quick on the uptake and makes a good student. Also, with his sense of fun and outgoing manner, he is likely to have many childhood friends. Life for the young Rat will be full of wonder, a round of constant discoveries.

As he matures, the Rat's engaging manner will bring him many admirers and an often active social life. However, although he is such attractive company and so popular, affairs of the heart can still bring him much anguish. He desires love but sometimes has difficulty in expressing his true feelings or allowing another to share his own private world. His reticence could cause many a promising romance to flounder, something he will feel deeply. However, when the Rat has found the person he considers to be his right partner, he will do his utmost to keep love alive, and will be loyal, protective and affectionate. To do well in life and feel fulfilled, the Rat does need a companion. He is not made for a more solitary lifestyle.

In his early adult years the Rat's work and material considerations can also bring him concern. Being so ambitious, he will
aspire to positions which may be either unrealistic or only
obtainable after much training and experience. Also, ever eager
to improve his situation, the Rat will feel constantly driven,
aiming to make the most of every opportunity and always on the
look-out for ways to advance. Sometimes he could overreach
himself and make mistakes and some painful errors of judgement. And the Rat does not take failure well!

Accordingly, his early working life, as he searches first for a
suitable career and then makes his mark, can be a difficult time.
If the Rat were prepared to proceed more steadily, building upon
his experience rather than constantly feeling he has to prove
himself, his progression could often be so much smoother as well
as more successful. He would also do better if he were to accept
his mistakes rather than regard them as a personal failure. While
no one likes failing, the Rat does have the ability to learn from
what happens and the resourcefulness to recover his ground.

Another of the Rat's concerns in his early adult years will be
money. He likes to live well and sometimes his indulgent nature
can lead him to spending more than he ought.

Life for the Rat in his early working years will not be easy, but
when he does find the right outlet for his talents and is better
able to control his restless spirit, he will come into his own and
can so often achieve the success and security he craves. His
later working life will often be that much more fulfilling for him.

As he progresses to older age, the Rat will often feel content
with what he has achieved and built up around him, as well as
enjoy the love and friendship of a great many. At this stage, with
grandchildren and even great-grandchildren, he is likely to be
part of a large family.

Life for the Rat will always be an interesting journey and
while he will hate the bumps along the way more than most, his

talents, ingenuity and charm will bring him many accomplishments of which he can truly be proud.

FAMOUS RATS

Ursula Andress, Louis Armstrong, Charles Aznavour, Lauren Bacall, James Baldwin, Shirley Bassey, Irving Berlin, Kenneth Branagh, Marlon Brando, Charlotte Brontë, George H. Bush, Glen Campbell, Dale Carnegie, David Carradine, Jimmy Carter, Maurice Chevalier, Aaron Copeland, Cameron Diaz, Benjamin Disraeli, David Duchovny, T. S. Eliot, Clark Gable, Hugh Grant, Geri Halliwell, Daryl Hannah, Thomas Hardy, Prince Harry, Nathaniel Hawthorne, Haydn, Charlton Heston, Buddy Holly, Mick Hucknall, Englebert Humperdink, Henrik Ibsen, Jeremy Irons, Jean-Michel Jarre, Danny Kaye, Gene Kelly, Lawrence of Arabia, Sir Andrew Lloyd Webber, Katherine Mansfield, Claude Monet, Richard Nixon, Sean Penn, Terry Pratchett, the Queen Mother, Burt Reynolds, Rossini, William Shakespeare, Yves St Laurent, Adlai Stevenson, Donna Summer, James Taylor, Leo Tolstoy, Henri Toulouse-Lautrec, Spencer Tracy, the Prince of Wales, George Washington, Dennis Weaver, the Duke of York, Emile Zola.

SUCCESS TIPS FOR THE RAT

Although the Rat is always eager to improve his lot he would do well to remember the 'Acres of Diamonds' story, recounted and made famous by Russell Conwell. In this true story a farmer sold his farm in order to go in search of diamonds. He failed. It was later discovered the farm he originally sold was just full of diamonds but the farmer had failed to recognize this. So the Rat should not always feel he has to go elsewhere looking for success, but consider building on what he has. His existing skills, experience and expertise count for a great deal and the Rat should make the most of them.

The Rat should also trust his own ideas and intuition more. He is very much an original thinker, but does not always make as much of his ideas and creative talents as he should. He should keep faith with himself and be more prepared to follow through some of his wonderful notions. It is said that success comes from within, and for the Rat this can be a very true. He is talented and resourceful, and he should make the most of his very considerable gifts.

The Rat possesses a highly inquisitive nature and likes to be involved in so much. However, by doing so he does run the risk of spreading his energies too widely. At times he will fare better by being more disciplined and concentrating on specific concerns. By focusing his attention better, the Rat will often achieve more as a result.

Although the Rat may be pleased to dispense advice to others, rarely does he confide in others or seek advice for himself. Despite his outgoing nature, he remains a very private and guarded individual. By talking and listening to those around him, though, he can often ease his concerns and also benefit from the advice he receives. At times the Rat really should be more open and trustful of others. He is a great communicator, but the communication must be two way!

The Rat would also do well to give more thought to his future. This includes being prepared to train for a better position, saving for the longer term and setting himself some objectives. The Rat may like to make the most of the present, but with thought and some careful planning, his future can be even more successful.

SOME FINAL THOUGHTS FROM RATS

I want to be all that I am capable of becoming.
Katherine Mansfield

Life is a great big canvas, and you should throw all the paint you
can on it.
Danny Kaye

The readiness is all.
William Shakespeare

Our doubts are traitors,
And make us lose the good we oft might win
By fearing to attempt.
William Shakespeare

An enterprise, when fairly once begun
Should not be left till all that ought is won.
William Shakespeare

Flaming enthusiasm, backed by horse sense and persistence, is
the quality that most frequently makes for success.
Dale Carnegie

Believe that you will succeed, and you will.
Dale Carnegie

Every individual has a place to fill in the world and is important
in some respect whether he chooses to be so or not.
Nathaniel Hawthorne

There are no gains without pains.
Adlai Stevenson

The world is before you and you need not take it or leave it as it was when you came in.
James Baldwin

Those who dream by night in the dusty recesses of their minds wake in the day to find that all was vanity; but the dreamers of the day are dangerous men, for they may act their dream with open eyes and make it possible.
Lawrence of Arabia

Everything comes if a man will only wait.
Benjamin Disraeli

I have brought myself by long meditation to the conviction that a human being with a settled purpose must accomplish it, and that nothing can resist a will which will stake even existence upon its fulfilment.
Benjamin Disraeli

The secret of success in life is for a man to be ready for his opportunity when it comes.
Benjamin Disraeli

The
Ox

Throughout the ages the Ox has worked dutifully, carrying out the tasks man has set. Whether toiling in fields or pulling ploughs, the Ox has proved a strong and faithful worker. And these qualities are so often found in those born under the second of the Chinese signs.

Above all, the Ox is reliable. True to his word, he is dependable and thorough and when he takes on a commitment he will see it through. He is methodical and tenacious and, unlike some, who may be tempted to start a welter of activities only to leave a lot unfinished, the Ox carefully chooses his tasks and will stick with them until they are complete.

The Ox is practical in nature, preferring tried and tested methods rather than new ways and concepts. He is a traditionalist, believing patience and sheer hard work will bring the results he wants. Napoleon Bonaparte, himself an Ox, once declared, 'Victory belongs to the most persevering,' and this does so capture the Ox philosophy. By remaining steadfast in the pursuit of his goals, he believes that success will ultimately come – and, for so many, it will.

With his determined and resolute approach, the Ox inspires confidence. Others respect him for his steadfast qualities. True, he may not be as flamboyant or showy as some, but he instils faith and it is for this reason that he is often able to rise to positions of power and authority. He is a leader and when people want results, the Ox will do his best to deliver.

In his manner, the Ox often appears quiet and reserved. He is never one for small talk or for idling away time in needless chatter. Neither is he one for frivolity. Instead, he simply prefers to get on with his own activities, preferably in his own way. He also likes to retain a certain independence and does not take kindly to too much interference or prying from others. The Ox is very much his own master.

However, if there is one aspect of his character that does let him down, it does tend to be his general interaction with others. The Ox is not a particularly keen or easy socializer and, in some cases, can lose out to those who may be more outgoing or make more effort to build up contacts. Also, by keeping his own counsel, the Ox can deny himself the chance of getting more help and input from others and this can sometimes hamper his progress. He may like to do things on his own, but he could benefit from a greater willingness to involve others.

The Ox can also be very set in his ways. He likes routine and following established patterns, and when his mind is made up, he is not one to change. He can be stubborn and sometimes pig-headed and this again is something that could cause him problems over the years.

Although the Ox may not appear ambitious, he is nevertheless keen to get results and make the most of his abilities. He prefers to specialize and once he has decided upon a career, he will aim to master its various aspects and work his way steadily through the ranks. As he does so, his conscientious and methodical approach will serve him well and help him to create a good impression. In addition, he is loyal, trustworthy and takes his responsibilities seriously. This allows others to put their faith in him and is another factor that can help him progress.

With his willingness to work hard and develop specialist skills, the Ox certainly has it within him to be successful in his chosen career and to earn a good living. However, he is not particularly acquisitive or materialistic. True, he will enjoy his comforts and particularly value the security that money can bring, but provided his needs and those of his loved ones are met, he will be content. Like most things in life, he will look after his money well and, when investing or saving, choose safe and proven routes rather than be tempted by more speculative or risky schemes. In later life, thanks to his often meticulous approach, the Ox can be materially well off.

The Ox attaches great value to his home and will devote much of his spare time to getting it as he wants. Being of a practical disposition, he will often do a lot of the work himself and will derive much pleasure from his accomplishments. The Ox also likes the outdoors and, where possible, will always try to ensure that he has a garden to tend. Again, he will get much satisfaction from this, particularly as he will be able to see the results of his work. Often the Ox will feel very content and at one with the world while out in his garden or, if a garden is not possible, out in the open air. If his work allows, he will generally prefer to live in the countryside or a small town rather than a bustling city.

The Ox will also make sure his home is run efficiently. Again, he likes to establish routine and order. Where others are concerned, this means that he likes to organize them. The Ox will certainly be dominant within his household, but he will also be most attentive. He will care deeply for his loved ones and will guide and advise them well. He is loyal and protective and a thoughtful provider. If he becomes a parent he will take his responsibilities seriously, doing all he can to help his children through their education as well as encourage them in their individual activities. The Ox is a good disciplinarian, but is kindly, caring and attentive.

As far as his social life is concerned, the Ox is likely to have a few close and select friends. Being quiet and often reserved, it does take him time to get to know others and indeed some of his closest friends are likely to date from his childhood years. He is not as keen as some on going out and is certainly not the most avid party-goer. However, with his carefully chosen friends, his family and his interests, the Ox will often be very content. He is not one for a flamboyant lifestyle or for putting on a show just for the sake of it. Indeed, the Ox is a sort of 'take me as you find me' character, unpretentious and down-to-earth, but very sincere and straightforward.

This attitude applies both to the male and female. However, of the two, the male is the more reserved and tends to keep his thoughts and feelings very much to himself. He has set ideas and ways and does not adapt that easily. However, while he is very much his own master and may not be a great communicator, he is considerate, caring and will never let anyone down. In appearance, when the situation calls for it, he can be smart and presentable, but when in the garden or carrying out some home project, he will not care one jot about how he looks! Instead, he will absorb himself totally in the activity he has set himself and while he is carrying it out will often be in a world of his own. The male Ox is highly practical and takes delight in making things and sorting out problems.

The female Ox is more outgoing than the male and more relaxed in the company of others. She is well liked and respected and expresses herself clearly, although, in typical Ox fashion, she is never one for idle chatter. She is a superb organizer and is highly efficient in the running and upkeep of her home. She is also very loyal and supportive to her loved ones. She has good dress sense, often preferring neat and practical outfits in keeping with her orderly manner.

Both the male and female Ox do have firm views and beliefs and once they have formed them, they do not tend to change them easily. Also, while the Ox has a calm and generally placid nature, should something rile him, then he is certainly capable of making his feelings known in no uncertain terms. The Ox does not often lose his temper, but when he does, it is something others are unlikely to forget for a long time. The anger of the Ox can be mighty indeed. Similarly, if someone tries to take advantage of him or lets him down, he will not readily forget it. The Ox sets high standards and is honourable in his dealings with others, and he expects others to follow suit.

As far as the Ox's personal interests are concerned, he prefers practical activities, especially carrying out projects on his home and garden. He is very adept in using his hands and will often enjoy making things or becoming expert in some sort of craft-work. In addition, he often has a good ear for music and will enjoy listening, playing and even composing.

According to tradition, Oxen born in winter and early spring will fare the best, but it is certain that the Ox, with his strong will, his determination and willingness to persevere, possesses the qualities that can lead to considerable success. By his own choosing, the road to success may be a long one, but it will be all the more certain and fulfilling as a result.

SUCCESS AND WORK

Despite his often quiet demeanour, the Ox possesses a steely resolve. He knows he has it within him to achieve a great deal and that through sheer tenacity and persistence, he will get the results he seeks. He is certainly not afraid of hard work or of taking on lengthy commitments. Indeed, if his chosen career requires a long apprenticeship or many exams to qualify, he is fully prepared to take this on.

The Ox is thorough in what he does. He is well organized and efficient and likes to establish a set pattern to his work. He is not one for frequent change or being in a too frenzied and turbulent atmosphere, but likes to get on with his duties and preferably be left to his own devices.

It is because the Ox is such a good worker and is prepared to take the time to master the various aspects of his work that he is able to rise to positions of seniority. Employers put their trust in him and colleagues their faith. Admittedly, the Ox may not be as outgoing or as pushy as some, but his resolve and commitment are greatly respected. When he finds himself in positions of authority he will take his responsibilities very seriously. Others will look up to him and depend upon him and they can be sure that he will do his best for everyone.

The Ox is certainly capable of achieving success in his work, but there are two factors that can tell against him. One is his unwillingness to embrace the new. Particularly in this age of rapid technological advance, the Ox should show more willingness to adapt to some of the ideas, concepts and tools that are now available. To remain too set in his ways could be damaging to his career prospects.

The other possible difficulty concerns his relations with his colleagues. Although always professional, the Ox sometimes lacks the personal touch and runs the risk of being labelled cool and aloof. He may not like wasting time in small talk, but sometimes a less formal approach can break barriers and be appreciated by others. Again, this is something the Ox would do well to bear in mind.

As a choice of career, in keeping with his strongly held beliefs, the Ox is often attracted to public service and politics, and in these areas he is certainly capable of making his mark. Also, being efficient and methodical, he is suited to administrative and managerial roles and, with his eye for detail and figures, he can be a meticulous banker, broker or financial adviser. With his willingness to study he could also be attracted to any other specialist areas which he feels are worthwhile and offer an interesting challenge, including the medical profession. Agriculture also suits the Ox.

The Ox can be gifted with his hands, whether in some technical or artistic role, and he could find this type of work satisfying, while the more creative Oxen can enjoy considerable success in the arts, particularly music.

The Ox is, though, not one who particularly enjoys travel and he should aim for a position which keeps him in one place rather than one which requires a lot of moving about.

Whatever the Ox chooses for a career, he will find that one of his greatest assets is his perseverance. This, combined with his patient manner, will often lead the Ox to the success and fulfilment he seeks.

SUCCESS AND MONEY

By nature the Ox is efficient and methodical and keeps a close watch over his financial position. Always aware of his outgoings and commitments, he budgets accordingly and will, as far as possible, keep his accounts balanced.

Although the Ox does appreciate the value of money, he is not materialistic. Rather than go off on lavish spending sprees, he prefers to plan his purchases. He is not greedy or over-indulgent. And if he has any money he does not immediately need, rather than be tempted to spend it, he will feel much more comfortable saving it, either for some specific purpose or for his more general future.

When saving, the Ox is not a speculator, often opting for secure savings schemes with a set return or, if investing in stocks, preferring well-established companies to a gamble on lesser-known ones. The Ox always prefers the traditional and proven. Thanks to his meticulous and careful approach, he will, over time, build up his savings so that in later years he will be reasonably well off.

The Ox is also a conscientious provider and will always make sure that his loved ones have all they need. While not being extravagant, he does aim for a good standard of living and a comfortable home, and in this he invariably succeeds admirably.

SUCCESS AND LOVE

Although love and romance are important to the Ox, they are not areas he finds particularly easy. With his independent and sometimes solitary nature, it does take him some time to build up a relationship and feel at ease with another person. He could also experience difficulty in coping with the emotions of love – he is, after all, not one for waxing lyrical or making flamboyant romantic gestures. Nor is he one for many romances or indeed one-night stands. He seeks a steady, meaningful and permanent relationship.

Those who get to know the Ox well will come to appreciate his sterling qualities, especially his kindly and caring nature. However, should a relationship flounder, the Ox can take it badly and it will take him a long time to recover and give his love to another. Some Oxen, particularly the males, may decide that rather than risk hurt again, they will devote themselves to their career and choose a more solitary lifestyle. Of the two, the female Ox will handle the emotions of the heart much better and with her quiet, confident and attractive manner, will not be short of admirers. And she does like to be flattered!

For the Ox to be happy in love, he needs to be less analytical at the start of any relationship. He should stop questioning his feelings and just let love take its course – and enjoy it! He needs to relax more and lose some of his reserve and seriousness. Although it may take him time to feel at ease with another, he must make an effort and at least show the warmth and richness of his character. If not, there is a danger these qualities will remain hidden and a prospective partner may in the end seek someone who is more responsive and expressive.

The Ox also tends to be set in his ways and should try to be more accommodating where others are concerned. Romance does call for adjustment and the Ox must be prepared to at least show willing.

If the Ox is prepared to enjoy and accept the wonders of love, even though it may throw him into so much turmoil, then he could find the course of love more interesting and a lot more successful. And the occasional gift and expression of his love will work wonders!

Courtship for the Ox can often be lengthy, but once he has found someone he wants to share his life with, he will be loyal, dependable and faithful. And if he chooses wisely, as most Oxen eventually do, then he can look forward to a close and enduring relationship.

SUCCESS WITH OTHERS

The Ox is quiet and reserved and because of this it does take him time to build up a satisfactory relationship with another. However once this has been established, it will often be lasting and beneficial. As the Ox will find, however, there are some signs he will get on better with than others.

⚞ With a Rat

The Ox can be very taken with the Rat's charm and warm personable nature, and relations between the two signs can be good.

In the parent–child relationship, the Ox parent will delight in the young Rat's versatile and resourceful nature and do much to support him as well as encourage him to use his many talents wisely. There will be a close bond between them.

As colleagues, the Ox and Rat recognize each other's strengths and will combine to good effect. The Ox will appreciate the Rat's ability to formulate and present ideas, as well as his masterful ways at PR! Together they make a successful team.

In love, the Ox and Rat are well suited. They both attach much importance to home and family life and will also benefit from each other's strengths. The Rat will help broaden the Ox's range of interests as well as encourage him to become more outgoing – and this, as the Ox will find, can make his life so much richer. This can be a close and successful relationship.

⚞ With another Ox

There will always be respect and understanding between two Oxen, but as both possess reserved and independent natures, in some situations a certain closeness could be lacking.

In the parent–child relationship, the Ox child will thrive in the secure and attentive atmosphere of an Ox household and will respond well to his Ox parent's guidance. Similarly, the parent will be especially fond of his child, seeing so much of himself in the young Ox and being able to steer him round some of the problems he may have experienced in his own formative years. It will be a beneficial relationship.

As colleagues, two Oxen will be hard-working and take their duties seriously. If they can agree on their individual roles, their combined efforts and sheer tenacity can lead them to considerable success. If not, their independent and sometimes self-willed ways could get the better of them and they could find themselves drifting apart.

In love, two Oxen will be loyal, devoted to their home and family, and will value the security and stability of their relationship. Their life together could, though, fall into something of a routine and lack the sparkle other relationships might have. But this should not bother an Ox couple too much.

With a Tiger

The Ox will care little for the outgoing and flamboyant ways of the Tiger and relations between them will be poor.

In the parent–child relationship, the Ox parent may marvel at the young Tiger's enterprising and resourceful nature, but also find him something of a handful! Always thirsting for new experiences and forever active, the young Tiger likes to live life fast – sometimes too fast for the more self-restrained Ox parent. Both can be strong-willed and this too will invariably lead to clashes. The pair will try hard to build accord and understanding, but this may not be easy.

As colleagues, relations will also be difficult, with the Ox considering the Tiger rash and impulsive. The Tiger likes action and plunging headfirst into activities, while the Ox is more of a planner. As both tend to be entrenched in their ways, agreement and understanding will be hard to find.

In love, relations will be challenging. The Ox seeks a quiet and stable existence and could find it difficult to adjust to the

Tiger's more active lifestyle. True, the Tiger is enjoyable company and an affectionate and generous partner, but these two signs live life at different speeds and often have different interests. This, combined with their strong wills and individualistic ways, does not augur well.

With a Rabbit

The Ox admires the quiet, placid and genial nature of the Rabbit and with many interests in common, these two signs get on well.

In the parent–child relationship, the Ox parent has great love and admiration for the quiet and good-natured Rabbit child. There will be a close bond between them, made all the stronger by the interests they share.

As colleagues, the Ox and Rabbit work well together and by combining their skills and strengths, they will often enjoy a good level of success. Both like order and method, and the Ox will especially appreciate the Rabbit's sound business sense and commercial acumen. They may not be risk takers, but through hard work and determination, their relationship will often be productive and profitable.

In love, the Ox and Rabbit can make a successful and happy match. They understand each other well and with similar values, outlooks and interests can become very close. Both yearn for a settled existence and attach great importance to their home life. The Ox will particularly delight in the Rabbit's companionable and affectionate nature. They will support each other and make an excellent match.

With a Dragon

Although the Ox has a high regard for the integrity and dynamism of the Dragon, there are many personality differences between them and, as a consequence, relations between the two signs can sometimes be tricky.

In the parent–child relationship, the Ox parent will delight in the young Dragon's inquisitive nature and keenness to learn, and will encourage him. However, the young Dragon does possess a mind of his own and the self-willed nature of both Dragon and Ox will give rise to some difficult moments.

As colleagues, the Ox and Dragon recognize and value their different strengths and can often work successfully together. The Ox particularly admires the resolve and enterprise of the Dragon and, as both are ambitious and diligent workers, between them they could go far.

In love, they will often intrigue each other and there could be considerable attraction in the early stages of a relationship, with the Ox enjoying the warmth and zest of an extrovert Dragon. But, over time, both could find it hard to change their ways, with the Ox preferring a quiet existence and the Dragon a more lively one. This, together with their strong wills and forceful natures, could lead to problems. Theirs can turn out to be a challenging match.

With a Snake

The Ox has much in common with the quiet and thoughtful Snake and these two signs get on well.

In the parent–child relationship, the Ox parent will encourage the Snake child and he in turn will draw strength from his confident and caring parent. The young Snake will benefit a great deal from the relationship and there will be a good rapport between parent and child.

As colleagues, the Ox and Snake make a powerful and successful combination. Both are careful planners and determined to make the most of themselves. They will trust and respect each other, with the Ox particularly valuing the Snake's commercial flair and judgement. They are also both of a patient disposition and are prepared to work long and hard to achieve their objectives.

In love, too, the Ox and Snake can make an excellent match. They both seek a calm, secure and settled home life and will often have interests they can share, including a fondness for the arts. There will be a good understanding between them and they will benefit from each other's strengths, with the Ox appreciating the quiet, considerate and affectionate ways of the Snake as well as his cultivated tastes and often gentle humour. A good and successful match.

With a Horse

The Ox and Horse are two redoubtable figures and it will not take too long before their strong wills and views clash. Relations between them are often difficult.

In the parent–child relationship, the Ox parent may admire the young Horse's thirst for knowledge and industrious nature, but with the child being lively and high-spirited, there could be some uncomfortable moments. Both may try, but relations between them will often be volatile.

As colleagues, both are hard workers and keen to progress, but given their different styles and the fact that each will want to prevail, agreement between them will be difficult. These two will prefer to stick to their own methods. Not a successful combination.

In love, these two powerful and resolute signs will have to make many adjustments if any match is to last. Both will try to dominate the relationship and compromise is not something that comes easily to either. They may recognize each other's strengths, with the Ox particularly appreciating the Horse's keen and positive spirit, but they live their lives at different speeds. It will take a special couple to make this relationship work.

✑ With a Goat

The Ox finds the Goat personality difficult to understand and relations between them will be poor.

In the parent–child relationship, the Ox parent may sometimes find it hard to get to grips with the young Goat's imaginative and often whimsical ways, but he will try to encourage and guide his child as best he can. The young Goat will value having such a supportive and protective parent. There may be differences between them, but with care and understanding, both will learn much from the other.

As colleagues, relations will be difficult, with their styles being very different. The Ox and Goat do not work well together.

In love, there will also be problems. The Ox, so careful, thorough and orderly, will soon become exasperated by the Goat's capricious ways. And by being his direct and forthright self, he will quickly upset the Goat's sensitive nature. In so many ways the Ox and Goat are complete opposites and it will take a very special couple to make the adjustments necessary to make the relationship work.

✑ With a Monkey

Although their personalities may be very different, the Ox has a great respect for the Monkey and relations between these two signs can be reasonable as well as often mutually beneficial.

In the parent–child relationship, the young Monkey may be mischievous and try the Ox parent's patience, but with his keen and earnest spirit the Ox parent will admire the young Monkey and teach him well. There will be a close bond between them.

As colleagues, the Ox and Monkey recognize that each is talented in different areas and they will combine their strengths to good effect. The Ox will particularly appreciate the Monkey's resourceful and enterprising spirit and with their joint ambition and drive, they can make a successful team.

In love, in spite of their many personality differences, the Ox and Monkey are often attracted to each other and can find much happiness. They will learn from each other, with the Monkey helping to make the Ox more outgoing as well as broadening his range of interests. There will be a good understanding between them and theirs can be a close and loving relationship.

✎ With a Rooster

The Ox admires the orderly and efficient Rooster and with similar interests, relations between the two signs will be good.

In the parent–child relationship, the Rooster child will look up to his quiet, kindly and attentive Ox parent and will strive hard to please. There will be a close and loving bond between them.

As colleagues, they will trust, respect and admire each other. They are both keen planners and are efficient and methodical. The Ox will be appreciative of the Rooster's drive and commitment, and they will make a successful and powerful combination.

In love, these two make a great match. Again their relationship will be helped by their shared outlook, as both are practical, well organized and have similar interests and values, including a fondness for the outdoors and for gardening. The Ox and Rooster will love each other dearly.

With a Dog

The Ox will respect the Dog's many fine qualities, but both possess a stubborn streak and as a result relations between them may not always be easy.

In the parent–child relationship, the Ox parent will encourage the young Dog, but may not always be fully appreciative of his sensitive nature. Relations between them will need to handled carefully and with consideration.

As colleagues, the Ox and Dog often have different outlooks, with Ox neither sharing the Dog's idealistic views nor having much patience with his more negative moods. These two will often prefer to work with someone more in tune with their own attitudes.

In love, both these signs are loyal and faithful and they can learn much from each other. The Ox will draw reassurance from the Dog's supportive manner as well as value his discreet and affectionate ways. However, the Ox may not always be so understanding when it comes to the Dog's worrying tendencies and sometimes his patience will wear thin. With understanding their relationship can work, but it will require effort and adjustments on both sides.

With a Pig

The Ox likes and respects the warm, friendly and genial Pig and relations between the two signs are invariably good.

In the parent–child relationship, the young Pig will respond well to his sincere and thoughtful Ox parent. There will be a good bond between them, made all the stronger by the many interests they share.

As colleagues, the Ox and Pig can achieve a good level of success. Both are scrupulous in their dealings and are prepared to work hard. They will combine their individual strengths well, with the Ox appreciating the Pig's enterprise and keen business sense.

In love, the Ox and Pig can make an excellent match. They both value a calm, harmonious and structured lifestyle and there will be much love and accord between them. They also have interests they can share, with both having a fondness for the outdoors. The Ox will benefit from the Pig's more outgoing and sociable nature and could become less intense as a result. These two can find much happiness together.

SUCCESS THROUGH LIFE

The Ox possesses a great sense of responsibility and this shows itself throughout his life. Always keen to do well, he advances steadily but surely. There will, though, be some stages on his life's journey that will be easier than others. The Ox will take any setbacks badly (he is a poor loser), but he is tenacious and his sheer will-power and strength of purpose will lead him on to many worthy accomplishments.

As a child the Ox will display from an early age a highly practical and determined nature. He will often be content playing by himself and will spend many hours building models, playing problem-solving games or mastering computer programs and bewildering others with his expertise! He will be quiet and not as outgoing as some, but has a strong will, which will inevitably lead to the odd confrontation with his seniors. He will have a small but particularly close band of friends, some of whom will remain friends for many years.

As he matures, the Ox will apply himself to his education. Rather than be an all-rounder, he tends to specialize in particular subjects, usually those of a more practical nature. Being methodical and conscientious, he is capable of securing some good qualifications, often ones which will be relevant to the career he wishes to take up. The Ox always likes to plan ahead.

As he enters the world of work, the Ox will invariably have a clear idea of what he wants to do. Sometimes he may be fortunate in quickly finding an opening he is suited for and once he has secured a position, he will stay there for some time, building on his experience, learning new skills and eventually seeking promotion, often within the same organization. The Ox does not like change and if feasible will stay with the same employer for some considerable time.

However, because of the condition of the employment market, some Oxen may initially have difficulty in getting a footing on the employment ladder in their chosen field. Once they do get a position, though, their determined and conscientious natures will invariably lead to them taking on more responsibilities, so setting them off on a pattern that will mark their working life – one of steady progression, often towards positions of authority.

The young Ox's career will often be successful, but his relations with those around him may be more difficult. It does take the Ox time to build up relationships and the affairs of the heart may not always go as smoothly as he would like. Should a romance fail, the hurt can linger for a long time. Accordingly, adolescence and early adulthood, when the pangs of love are often so strong, are not easy times emotionally for the Ox. However, if he can learn to be more at ease in the company of others, he could find his relations with those around him generally so much happier.

Once the Ox has found a partner to share his life with, he will be loyal, caring and dependable. He is, after all, never one to enter into a commitment lightly. Similarly, if he becomes a parent, he will be attentive, aiming to set a good example and guiding his children with kindness as well as just the right level of discipline. Family life is often a central part of the Ox's life. However, again, should the relationship with his partner fail, it will hit the Ox hard and it will be a long time before he feels able to trust again.

The Ox's later years will often see him financially secure and able to enjoy the results of his labour. However, the older Ox could sometimes be a lonely figure. He may not know many outside his immediate circle and his social life could be almost non-existent. Oxen who find themselves in such a position will need to draw on their practical natures and take action. Although they may not be keen, they should force themselves to go out and meet others, maybe at a local club, society or some other social gathering. By making the effort, the older Ox will often be able to add a new and meaningful dimension to his life, one which could have been missing for some time.

Throughout his life, so much depends on the Ox's attitude, but he certainly has it within him to achieve a great deal. If he is able to manage his relations with others, then his life can really be one of success and happiness.

FAMOUS OXEN

Robert Altman, Hans Christian Andersen, Johann Sebastian Bach, Warren Beatty, Napoleon Bonaparte, Albert Camus, Jim Carrey, Barbara Cartland, Charlie Chaplin, Melanie Chisholm, George Clooney, Jean Cocteau, Natalie Cole, Bill Cosby, Tom Courtenay, Tony Curtis, Diana, Princess of Wales, Marlene Dietrich, Walt Disney, Patrick Duffy, Jane Fonda, Gerald Ford, Edward Fox, Michael J. Fox, Peter Gabriel, Richard Gere, William Hague, Handel, King Harald V of Norway, Adolf Hitler, Dustin Hoffman, Oliver Wendell Holmes, Anthony Hopkins, William James, Billy Joel, Don Johnson, Lionel Jospin, King Juan

Carlos of Spain, Mark Knopfler, Burt Lancaster, k. d. Lang, Jessica Lange, Jack Lemmon, Alison Moyet, Eddie Murphy, Paul Newman, Jack Nicholson, Leslie Nielsen, Billy Ocean, Gwyneth Paltrow, Oscar Peterson, Colin Powell, Robert Redford, Lionel Richie, Rubens, Meg Ryan, Carl Schurz, Jean Sibelius, Sissy Spacek, Bruce Springsteen, Rod Steiger, Meryl Streep, Lady Thatcher, Henry David Thoreau, Dick van Dyke, Vincent van Gogh, the Duke of Wellington, W. B. Yeats.

SUCCESS TIPS FOR THE OX

The Ox is a very down-to-earth character, unpretentious and straightforward. However, while others may admire and respect him for what he is and stands for, he sometimes lets himself down in his dealings with others. He tends to keep his views and feelings to himself and is not an easy socializer. This is something the Ox should aim to improve. He should try to become more relaxed and responsive in the company of others and while he may not like idle chatter, he should give more time to pleasantries and learn to display the warmer and friendlier aspects of his character, which may otherwise remain hidden to all but a few. He can learn so much from meeting and exchanging views with others, and he should this do more often. The Ox has so much to give, but more attention to PR would certainly not come amiss!

The Ox takes his responsibilities seriously and he drives himself hard. However, he should make sure his life does not become all work and no play. It would do him good to unwind properly and enjoy himself. If he can learn to relax more as well as add some variety into his life, he will feel so much better for it. He works hard, but he should make sure he savours the fruit of his labours!

The Ox also tends to get entrenched in his ways and there will be times when he would do better by showing more flexibility. He should not be so distrustful of change and should aim to embrace the new a little more readily, otherwise he could find himself losing out to those more prepared to adapt.

The Ox does not like failing in what he sets out to do and rather than risk failure, he sometimes holds back from taking chances or testing his often very good ideas. Again, if he were to be less reticent, he could enjoy a greater level of success and find what he does more fulfilling as a result. As Oliver Wendell Holmes, himself an Ox, wrote, 'Many people die with their music still in them.' The Ox has so much to give that he should be prepared to go after what he wants. By doing so, he will find his life will be much more rewarding.

Every so often the Ox should make it his policy to develop himself in some way, perhaps by learning a new skill, taking up a different interest or reading up on a certain subject. By extending his skills and broadening his knowledge, he will not only open up new doors for himself but also find new possibilities emerging as well. The Ox must never stop developing, for this is the way of progress – and success.

SOME FINAL THOUGHTS FROM OXEN

To know oneself, one should assert oneself.
Albert Camus

All our dreams can come true, if we have the courage to pursue them.
Walt Disney

Greatness is not in where we stand, but in what direction we are moving. We must sail sometimes with the wind and sometimes against it – but sail we must, and not drift, not lie at anchor.
Oliver Wendell Holmes

The truest wisdom is a resolute determination.
Napoleon Bonaparte

Ideals are like stars; you will not succeed in touching them with your hands. But like the seafaring man on the desert of waters, you choose them as your guides, and following them you will reach your destiny.
Carl Schurz

I will act as if what I do makes a difference.
William James

I am in earnest – I will not equivocate – I will not excuse – I will not retreat a single inch; and I will be heard.
William Lloyd Garrison

I do not know anyone who has got to the top without hard work. That is the recipe. It will not always get you to the top, but it should get you pretty near.
Margaret Thatcher

One only gets to the top rung on the ladder by steadily climbing up one at a time, and suddenly all sorts of powers, all sorts of abilities which you thought never belonged to you, suddenly become a possibility and you think, 'Well, I'll have a go, too.'
Margaret Thatcher

Within you there is a stillness and sanctuary to which you can
retreat at anytime and be yourself.
Hermann Hesse

Live your beliefs and you can turn the world around.
Henry David Thoreau

I have learned that if one advances in the direction of his
dreams, and endeavours to live the life he has imagined, he will
meet with a success unexpected in common hours.
Henry David Thoreau

Men are born to success, not to fail.
Henry David Thoreau

The
Tiger

With his distinctive appearance, stealth and power, the Tiger commands respect and attention. And those born under the third Chinese sign are destined to impress, often leading full and eventful lives.

Tigers are born under the sign of courage and are bold, active and enterprising. The Tiger is also blessed with luck and in the East it is considered that in the home the Tiger can help reduce the risk of thieves, fire and evil spirits.

The Tiger tends to live for the moment and whenever he devotes himself to some undertaking or cause, he will give it his complete attention. He is never half-hearted. He is honourable in his dealings with others and has a particular dislike of the use of devious means to achieve results. Instead the Tiger relies on his own abilities and his commanding personality, as well as his often innovative approach, to get his way. He knows how to impress and throughout his life his qualities can help him to achieve some wonderful successes. However, the Tiger can sometimes be his own worst enemy and possesses trails which, unless watched, can undermine him.

In particular the Tiger can be reckless. In his haste and eagerness, he can take too many risks, cut too many corners or take
action without thinking of the consequences. At times he can be
just too impulsive. Similarly, in his desire for results, the Tiger
does not always pay attention to the finer details of his actions
and sometimes this too can leave him exposed and derail his
plans. If the Tiger were to plan better, then he would find his
level of success that much greater.

Another of the Tiger's failings is that in his desire to lead, he
does not like taking orders from others or paying too much attention to their advice. Instead he likes to be his own master, setting
about his activities in his own way, and sometimes his obstinacy
and over-reliance on himself work against him.

Because of his often self-willed nature and readiness to take
risks, the Tiger's life will certainly contain many peaks and
troughs. However, the Tiger is quick to learn from his experiences – and here the school of hard knocks will teach him some
valuable lessons – and his unquenchable spirit and optimistic
nature will drive him forward. There will be times when the Tiger
is knocked down, but he will invariably bounce back!

The Tiger is also versatile. He has wide interests and likes to
be involved in whatever is going on around him. Indeed, he is
rarely still. He will always be keen to discover more about a new
idea, product or craze. However, while he can for a time become
totally immersed in a new hobby or interest, he may not
continue it for long. The Tiger is continually thirsting for new
experiences and challenges.

In his lifetime the Tiger will have many different interests, but
one which will be paramount will be his love of travel. He very
much enjoys visiting different areas, particularly the more
unusual and remote, and he will find that travel does much to
satisfy his adventurous spirit. He can also be fond of sport,
especially following or becoming involved in those activities

which offer excitement and some sort of personal challenge. The Tiger is, after all, keen on action and not averse to risk.

The Tiger also possesses a fine imagination and will enjoy activities which allow him to develop his ideas, maybe through writing, painting, designing or in some other sphere that allows him to be creative and express himself. Whatever his interest, he can be a true original and some Tigers have achieved considerable success by turning a skill to a vocation.

In his work, the Tiger does have much to offer. Enthusiastic, enterprising and so full of ideas, he likes to be at the forefront of activity. With his competitive spirit, he is keen to make the most of himself and to take the lead. He is a fine worker and cares deeply about his reputation. He is not one to take criticism or a slur on his character lightly. However, the Tiger can himself risk undermining his position by being too impulsive or taking one risk too many. Also, his staying power is not always that good and while he might start a project with tremendous enthusiasm, once his interest starts to wane or he sees something that looks more appealing, he will quickly change course. If he were prepared to show more long-term commitment and take the time to build on his accomplishments, he would sometimes achieve a lot more.

Also, while the Tiger does like to play a major part in all he does, when major decisions need to be taken he can appear indecisive. At such times, he would find it helpful to be more open to advice rather than keep his own counsel.

The Tiger does, though, have a very likeable personality. He can be witty, charming and fun to be with, and he has a genuine interest in others. He is sincere, open in his views and has a profound dislike of any sort of pretension or falsehood. He is also generous and loyal, both to family and friends. With his wide interests and outgoing nature, he will have a large social circle, often drawn from many different walks of life. He enjoys an active social life and as well as being a keen party-goer could be an active member of an interest group or society.

In addition, the Tiger does have a genuine interest in the welfare of others and can be very public-spirited. Many Tigers are willing to give their time to support some humanitarian cause or assist the community in some way. Also, if the Tiger feels a certain injustice has been done or that his efforts can help others, then he is often prepared to put his weight behind some cause or campaign. With his fine and sometimes rebellious spirit, he makes a redoubtable campaigner, especially against authority.

As he likes to keep so active, the Tiger is not one for spending a great deal of time at home and will, over the years, change his residence many times. Although he may not be the keenest on housework, considering that there are far more interesting things to do, his home will be comfortable, orderly and stylish. Here again the Tiger will show his flair for choosing the distinctive, using colour and light to good effect as well as adorning his home with many wonderful souvenirs that he has picked up on his travels. The Tiger's home will be well run and stamped with his vibrant personality.

In his household, the Tiger will certainly be the instigator of much that goes on. Home life for him (and others) will often be busy. The Tiger tends to marry young and as a partner will be caring, protective and generous. He also makes an excellent and responsible parent and will take a keen interest in the education of his children. With his generally enthusiastic nature and wide interests, he certainly knows how to stimulate the imagination of the young and makes a fine teacher.

In some signs, the personality differences between the male and female are marked, but it is not so with the Tiger. Both male and female have a mind of their own, possess fine and strong spirits and keep themselves busy with a whole range of interests and activities. And while society sometimes has particular roles laid out for men and women, the Tiger will quite happily break with convention and just forge ahead. The Tiger is always a rebel and a pioneer.

Both the male and female Tiger can be most striking in their appearance. Some, keen to keep up with the new, will be particularly fashion conscious and will prepared to be adventurous (and sometimes daring) in what they wear, while others will choose to have their own style. Whether this is smart and elegant, casual or even eccentric, the Tiger will often be distinctive.

Tigers born at night tend to be calmer and more disciplined than those born during daylight hours, but all possess the talents and personality to make much of their life. If the Tiger can keep the more reckless aspects of his character in check, then his often eventful life can be crowned with some really worthy achievements.

SUCCESS AND WORK

Energetic, enthusiastic and full of ideas, the Tiger is certain to make an impression. He is quick-witted and alert and is prepared to work hard. He does not shirk responsibility, likes to be at the forefront and can be an inspiring leader or manager. He leads by example and will often make an impact. He also possesses a strong sense of integrity and will be honourable in his dealings with others. However, he does have a competitive spirit and is certainly never afraid to take on opposition if there is something to be gained by it.

The Tiger is also prepared to take risks and while these will often work out well, there will be occasions when his judgement is wrong and he will have to learn from bitter experience. Although suffering deeply, he will often gain a great deal from his setbacks and, after a time, his zeal and determined spirit will re-emerge and he will apply himself to new challenges. As the Chinese proverb states, 'If you get up one more time than you fall, you will make it through.' The Tiger is certainly prepared to get up that one more time.

In his early adult years the Tiger will try his hand at many different jobs. While he may start some of these full of enthusiasm, he could find that after a time his interest starts to wane and he will decide to try something else. In his early working life, he often lacks staying power and will frequently change his job. He is also poor at taking orders and this is something he will need to address in the early stages of his career. The young Tiger may think he knows best, but others (including his superiors) may not always agree.

In his work the Tiger does need to be able to express himself and if he finds himself in a too restrictive a position or feels that his ideas and talents are being stifled, his rebelliousness and restlessness will soon emerge. A thwarted or frustrated Tiger can be difficult indeed. It is for this reason that some Tigers will choose the route of self-employment, so that they can be their own master, or even drop out of the employment market for a time.

The Tiger will find that he is often suited to careers in sales, marketing, commerce and the media, all of which will allow him to use his ideas and creative flair to good effect. He will also enjoy positions that allow him to travel and meet others. In addition, he makes a fine campaigner and advocate and can be effective when working for causes which interest him and which he feels can benefit others. This includes charitable and humanitarian work or, with the Tiger's sense of justice and fair play, the police and legal professions. Possessing such an inventive mind, he can also enjoy success in the arts and, being able to communicate so well, he makes an excellent and inspiring teacher.

The Tiger certainly has the talents and personality to do well. However, in order to realize his potential, he needs to overcome his restlessness and the temptation to keep chopping and changing. By building up his skills and expertise, he is capable of making his mark in the career he finally does choose.

SUCCESS AND MONEY

The Tiger has a very enterprising nature and by using his talents to good effect, he has it in him to earn a good income. However, he likes to live for the moment and his predisposition to run risks and make impulsive decisions can sometimes result in financial disasters, or at least sizeable dents in his resources. In addition, the Tiger likes to spend and is generous towards others, and sometimes his money will come and go all too easily. As a result, there is bound to be at least one period in the Tiger's life when he finds himself struggling financially or suffers a reversal in fortune, often because of some misjudgement. Here again, experience will teach the Tiger some painful lessons – but he will learn well.

In money matters the Tiger should aim to give more thought to the long term. If he wishes to have a comfortable retirement, he needs to save regularly and ideally should have a plan or policy which he can build up over the years. In addition, he would find it helpful to exercise greater control over his level of spending. Sometimes he yields to temptation all too readily and does not always put his money to its best use. If the Tiger wishes to be more successful in money matters, then he does need to watch his outgoings as well as make more provision for the future. Also, should he ever be tempted to commit his money to any particularly risky venture, he should make sure he checks the implications thoroughly and obtains proper advice. Without vigilance, he could find certain schemes do not work out as he had envisaged and again he will come to regret his haste.

However, while the Tiger's fortunes can fluctuate quite widely, with care and judicious use of his talents, he is certainly capable of enjoying prosperity. In addition, he is blessed with a fair amount of luck – although he must always avoid pushing this too far.

SUCCESS AND LOVE

The Tiger is passionate and romantic and does so enjoy being in love. As with so many aspects of his life, when in love he throws his heart and soul into it and enjoys it to the full. A Tiger in love is a Tiger in bliss.

As he is outgoing and sociable, the Tiger makes friends with ease and will have many admirers and countless romances. He will particularly enjoy the early stages of a romance, wondering just where it will lead and what is in store. In his usual optimistic way, he will be full of hope, desire and expectation, only for this sometimes to be dashed. The early and often heady days of romance will be hard to maintain and sometimes the Tiger will have to accept that this relationship was just not meant to be and start the quest all over again. He will certainly have many romances and his love life will contain some wonderfully happy times, though also times of disappointment.

When the Tiger does find someone with whom he wishes settle down – and he often chooses to marry young – he will give this person his commitment and trust and be as generous and supportive as any. In return, he will want his partner to share in his hopes and ideas as well as become involved in his multitude of interests. The Tiger is not one for staying still. He seeks an active lifestyle and expects his partner to follow suit. Some of the quieter and more introverted signs could find the pace just too much and it is for this reason that the Tiger should make sure his partner is prepared to understand and to some extent adapt to his ways. If not, he will become stifled and restless and the relationship may flounder. To prevent this, the Tiger should take the time to really get to know his prospective partner rather than enter into a commitment too hurriedly. That way the relationship is more likely to endure.

The most ideal partner for the Tiger will be someone who is similarly outgoing and adventurous as well as most supportive. In return, that person can look forward to a most interesting and often rewarding time ahead – life is rarely dull with an active Tiger about!

SUCCESS WITH OTHERS

Sincere, sociable and interesting to be with, the Tiger makes popular company. He is genuinely interested in others and enjoys conversation. However, there are some signs he can relate to far better than others.

With a Rat

The Tiger enjoys the company of the lively and sociable Rat and the two get on well.

In the parent–child relationship, the Tiger parent will do much to encourage the young Rat in his many interests as well as delight in his resourceful and responsive manner. There is a good rapport between them, although the young Rat may sometimes crave a more settled existence than is usually found in the active Tiger household.

As colleagues, the often brilliant ideas of these two make them a great team. Ambitious, enthusiastic and resourceful, they have a lot in their favour and by combining their strengths can achieve considerable success.

In love, there will be much passion between the Tiger and Rat. They have many interests they can share and will support each other well. The Tiger will be particularly won over by the Rat's charm, resourcefulness and ability as a homemaker. However, their different attitudes towards money – the Tiger being more generous and liberal than the Rat – as well as the Tiger's more restless nature could give rise to problems. Generally, though, with understanding and effort, these two can make a reasonably good match.

With an Ox

With such a different lifestyle and outlook, the Tiger will not find the Ox easy company and relations between them will be difficult.

In the parent–child relationship, the Tiger parent will admire the young Ox's conscientious and dutiful manner and will guide him well. However, the Ox child prefers a quiet and stable existence and could feel ill at ease with a lively and outgoing Tiger parent and the buzz of activity that so characterizes a Tiger household.

As colleagues, again their different outlooks will cause problems. The Tiger will regard the Ox as an inhibiting influence, particularly as the Ox does not share his adventurous and pioneering ways. With their strong and self-willed natures, clashes are inevitable and these two will prefer to go their separate ways.

In love, they may recognize each other's qualities and the Tiger will particularly admire the Ox's quiet, conscientious and sincere manner. However, the Tiger is so much more active and outgoing than the Ox that their different interests, lifestyles and tastes will be difficult to reconcile. This will be a challenging match.

With another Tiger

When two Tigers get together, their competitive and strong-willed natures invariably get the better of them. Each will try to dominate and relations between them will be tricky.

In the parent–child relationship, the Tiger parent will do much to encourage the young Tiger's inquisitive nature and will teach him well. They will have many interests they can share and enjoy, but the young Tiger does have a mind of his own and does not like obeying orders (a typical Tiger trait!) and this will inevitably lead to confrontation. Parent and child will love each other, but relations will be volatile.

As colleagues, two Tigers will have ideas aplenty, but each will want to take the lead. Their competitive, independent and self-willed natures will get the better of them and rather than co-operate or compromise, each will prefer to seek the success they want in their own way rather than work together.

In love, again the prospects are not good. Lively, sociable and fun-loving the Tiger may be, but he is also restless and likes to dominate. So each Tiger will want to hold sway and when disagreements emerge, their frank and forthright natures will get the better of them. Two Tigers do not live happily under the same roof. They are too vibrant, too volatile and too strong-willed to live in harmony and a match between them will require enormous care and understanding if it is to stand any chance of success.

✎ With a Rabbit

Although different in so many respects, the Tiger has a great respect for the genial Rabbit and relations between them will often be beneficial.

In the parent–child relationship, the Tiger parent will do much to build up the Rabbit child's confidence and self-belief and while the child may not always like the high levels of activity found in a Tiger household, there will be a good level of understanding between parent and child.

As colleagues, the Tiger and Rabbit have a fine regard for each other's skills and strengths and by combining these can make a fine and often successful team. The Tiger will particularly respect the Rabbit's good business sense as well as benefit from his more organized and disciplined approach. Between them, these two have qualities and ideas that can take them far.

In love, there is often considerable passion between the Tiger and Rabbit. The Tiger will be very taken with the Rabbits's quiet yet discreet and companionable manner. They relate well to each other and will have many interests they can share, including leading an often active social life. These two will learn much from each other and make a good match.

✎ With a Dragon

Lively, dynamic and outgoing, the Tiger enjoys the Dragon's company. Admittedly there will be times when their views and self-willed natures will clash, but there will be a good deal of respect between them.

In the parent–child relationship, the Tiger parent will admire the young Dragon's enthusiastic nature and with many interests they can share, there will be a great bond between them.

As colleagues, these two are bold, enterprising and resourceful. Recognizing each other's strengths, they will combine their talents and work well together. However, they are often in a hurry for results and if tempted to take too many risks, their good work could so easily be undone. With care and luck, though, they could be bound for very great success.

In love, there will be passion, excitement and so much to share. The Tiger will particularly appreciate the Dragon's sincere, confident and outgoing manner and will find him a loyal and lively companion. These two live life to the full. However, both like to dominate and have a tendency to speak their minds. Ideally, to prevent too much disagreement, they should decide who does what in their household and have a clear division of responsibility. But, despite the occasional rocky moment, these two can make an exciting match.

With a Snake

The Tiger, who is so open and upfront, will find it hard to understand the reserved and guarded Snake. Relations between them will be difficult.

In the parent–child relationship, relations will need to be handled with care. For the Tiger, a child should be brimming with energy and constantly active, and he will find the reflective and sometimes solitary ways of a Snake child a mystery. But for all this, the Tiger, recognizing the young Snake's ability and often keen intellect, will teach him well and try to make him more outgoing.

As colleagues, there will be a distinct lack of trust and understanding between these two. Their approaches are so different and each will be loathe to co-operate with or adjust to the other. The outgoing and adventurous Tiger will find it hard to accept the Snake's more cautious and guarded manner and will wonder what the Snake may be up to. In the workplace these two will quickly go their separate ways.

In love, the Tiger may for a time be intrigued by the Snake's quiet and alluring manner, but the Tiger likes activity while the Snake prefers a gentler pace, the Tiger is generous with his money while the Snake is careful, the Tiger is restless while the Snake likes stability, and so it goes on. There are just so many differences between the two that relations between them will be fraught with difficulty.

With a Horse

The Tiger has a great admiration for the Horse and with their lively natures and much in common, relations between them will be good.

In the parent–child relationship, the Tiger parent will admire the young Horse's willing and adventurous spirit. Both keen to learn and be involved in so much, parent and child will enjoy a great rapport.

As colleagues, both are keen to get results and are industrious, enterprising and ambitious. The Tiger will find reassurance in such a redoubtable ally and together they will achieve a great deal. The Horse and Tiger make a very successful combination.

In love, there will be passion, excitement and just so much to share. These two are forever active and between them will have a whole range of interests and activities to fill their time. Keen socializers and travellers, they will enjoy life to the full. Admittedly, their forthright natures may sometimes get the better of them and their strong wills will clash, but they will mean a great deal to each other and make a successful and lively match.

With a Goat

The Tiger thinks well of the genial and easy-going Goat and relations between them can be good.

In the parent–child relationship, relations will be tricky however. The young Goat is quiet and sensitive and while he may love his Tiger parent dearly, the Tiger's dominant nature and expectations can sometimes be a bit too much. The young Goat needs a lot of gentle encouragement and support which the Tiger must be prepared to give if relations between them are to be good.

As colleagues, the Tiger and Goat are both creative and if their work allows them to use their talents, they can achieve great success. The Tiger will quite happily take the lead in any venture and will have a high regard for the Goat's input and ideas. However, both tend to be less disciplined when dealing with money matters and here care will be needed.

In love, the Tiger and Goat can find much happiness. Passionate and fun-loving, these two will have great times together. The Tiger will particularly value the Goat's caring, affectionate and supportive nature as well as share many of his interests. Provided they can control their spendthrift tendencies – and are not permanently in debt! – these two can make a good match.

With a Monkey

The Tiger may for a time find the Monkey interesting and enjoyable company, but their competitive natures and personality differences will eventually get the better of them.

In the parent–child relationship, relations will generally be positive. The Tiger parent will admire the young Monkey's resourceful and adventurous spirit and while sometimes the young Monkey may push the Tiger's patience too far, there will be a good bond between them.

As colleagues, both the Tiger and Monkey may be enterprising and have plenty of ideas, but each will want to take the lead. Also, the Tiger may have misgivings about the Monkey's approach and certainly will have no truck with the Monkey's more cunning (and sometimes devious) notions. With this lack of trust and understanding, they do not make a successful combination.

In love, the Tiger may be enchanted by the Monkey's sense of fun and his lively spirit, but when they get to know each other better, problems will soon emerge. The Monkey likes to keep tabs on most things and the Tiger could come to resent his inquisitive nature. He does, after all, like a certain amount of freedom and independence. With each being strong-willed and wanting to hold sway, compromise and agreement could sometimes be difficult. A challenging match.

With a Rooster

Although there is much about the Rooster that the Tiger will admire, their forceful and forthright natures will cause problems between them. Relations will be difficult.

In the parent–child relationship, the Tiger parent will be proud of the young Rooster's keen and industrious manner, but both can be stubborn and forthright and there will be some mighty clashes of will. Also, the young Rooster, who so appreciates order and planning, may not feel at ease with the Tiger parent's impulsive nature. They will try and they will have their truces, but these two will also have their more difficult moments.

As colleagues, each could benefit from the other's strengths. In particular the Tiger could gain from the Rooster's more methodical and tenacious approach. However, both are competitive and forthright, and as each will want to take the lead and set about activities in their own way, clashes will result. If they can accommodate their differences, between them they have the strengths to achieve great success, but so much depends on their willingness to co-operate. And it will not be easy.

In love, these two lively and sociable signs can initially get on well. There will be passion, fun and so much hope for the future. But the long-term prospects are more difficult. Both are candid, both like to have their own way and the Tiger's restless and impulsive nature will be at odds with the Rooster's desire for order, planning and set routine. If they can reconcile their differences and allow each other the freedom and space they both need, then it is just possible a match between them could work, but it will require a special effort ... and a special couple.

With a Dog

The Tiger likes and respects the Dog and there will be a good understanding between them.

In the parent–child relationship, the Dog child will learn much from his supportive Tiger parent. The Tiger will boost the Dog's confidence, give him reassurance and raise his self-esteem. The young Dog will respond well and work hard to please his Tiger parent. There will be much love between them.

As colleagues, these two also get on well. With the Tiger's inventiveness and Dog's more considered approach, they are a successful combination. The Tiger will particularly value the Dog's high standards as well as his judgement. Together these two can go far.

In love, the Tiger and Dog will support each other well. Both are loyal and trusting and the restless and often impulsive Tiger will become more settled with a dutiful and caring Dog as a partner. They will have many interests they can share and, as both are idealists, could unite in championing some cause in which they passionately believe. The Tiger and Dog are good for each other and make an excellent match.

With a Pig

The Tiger finds the Pig enjoyable company and with many interests in common and a fondness for the good life, these two get on well.

In the parent–child relationship, the young Pig will develop well with a caring but imaginative Tiger parent. The Pig child will gain in confidence and seek to emulate his enterprising parent. There will be a good bond between them.

As colleagues, their enterprise and often innovative approach can serve them well. The Tiger will particularly value the Pig's good business sense and commercial acumen. However, to maximize their potential, they do need to remain disciplined and have a common purpose.

In love, there will be passion aplenty. These two will love each other dearly and each will learn from the other. The Tiger in particular will benefit from the Pig's often wise counsel and could become less rash and impulsive as a result. Both like to live life to the full. They make a good match.

SUCCESS THROUGH LIFE

As the Tiger likes to keep himself so active, his life will often be eventful and sometimes, because of his restless nature, volatile too. In each of the stages of the Tiger's life, he will want to do a great deal and accordingly will have much to learn. Experience will teach him well.

As a child, the Tiger's lively and spirited nature will soon show itself and the young Tiger will delight in a multitude of different interests and activities. Always eager to experiment, he will be a quick learner. However, his boisterous and energetic nature and high spirits will sometimes lead him into awkward predicaments. In addition, he is not one for rules and regulations and his rebellious and self-willed tendencies will bring him into conflict with others. One moment life will be full of joy and happiness, the next pandemonium. If the young Tiger were prepared to be more compliant and accept the reasons behind some of the instructions given him, he would find life much easier and more enjoyable as a result.

The Tiger often chooses to leave home and break away from parental authority at an early age. Full of hope, enthusiasm and energy, he will be eager to make his mark, enjoying the freedom adulthood can bring as well as following through his ideas and aspirations. Here again, however, life will teach the Tiger some hard lessons. Despite his commendable spirit, not all will work out as he would like. Workwise, his restless and ambitious spirit will be always urging him to try for different and better positions and, despite some achievements, he could feel unfulfilled and frustrated. Indeed, it is these feelings that have led many Tigers to opt out for a while and pursue their own destiny, irrespective of the consequences. Whether travelling round the world or abandoning everything to follow a dream, the Tiger is, at some time, prepared to take the risk. His desires may mean he will have to grapple with financial problems and a general lack of resources. Fortunately, in many cases, his enterprise and resourcefulness will come to his rescue, but financially some years can turn out to be precarious.

On a personal level, too, the Tiger's early adult life could be turbulent. There will be romance and so much fun – but there could also be heartache. To prevent mistakes being made, the Tiger would do well to let relationships build up gradually rather than be so ready to rush into a sometimes hasty commitment.

Again, it is a case of not letting his impulsive nature get the better of him.

However, as the Tiger matures and benefits from his experiences, he will find himself at last becoming more focused on what he wants to do as well as taking his responsibilities (especially towards his loved ones and parenthood) seriously. By channelling his energies and talents in a more focused way, he will find himself at last enjoying the achievements he has worked so hard to obtain. However, his keen and adventurous spirit will always remain with him and sometimes after climbing one pinnacle of success, the Tiger will try for another, with some Tigers choosing to change career in their later years. The Tiger does like challenges, even though at the time they may give him (and his loved ones) some uncomfortable moments. He does need to pursue his destiny, even though this may sometimes mean throwing caution to the wind.

With his active lifestyle, the Tiger can be prone to accidents and does not always reach old age. But the many that do will still often turn their attention to new (if slightly less energetic) pursuits, as well as follow the activities of family members with much pride. The mature Tiger will probably have regrets about some of the things he may not have achieved or undertaken, but rather than dwell on these, he should look back on the incredible journey his own life has been and at the great deal he has actually done. The Tiger will certainly have packed more into his years than a great many others and will have had numerous adventures.

FAMOUS TIGERS

Debbie Allen, Kofi Annan, Sir David Attenborough, Queen Beatrix of the Netherlands, Victoria Beckham, Beethoven, Tony

Bennett, Tom Berenger, Chuck Berry, Jon Bon Jovi, Sir Richard Branson, Emily Brontë, Mel Brooks, Isambard Kingdom Brunel, Agatha Christie, Charlotte Church, Phil Collins, Sheryl Crow, Tom Cruise, Charles de Gaulle, Leonardo DiCaprio, Emily Dickinson, Dwight Eisenhower, Queen Elizabeth II, Enya, Roberta Flack, E. M. Forster, Frederick Forsyth, Jodie Foster, Connie Francis, James A. Froude, Crystal Gayle, Elliott Gould, Buddy Greco, Ed Harris, Hugh Hefner, Stan Laurel, Jay Leno, Groucho Marx, Karl Marx, John Masefield, Marilyn Monroe, Demi Moore, Alanis Morissette, Marco Polo, Beatrix Potter, Renoir, Kenny Rogers, the Princess Royal, Dame Joan Sutherland, Dylan Thomas, Liv Ullman, Jon Voight, Julie Walters, H. G. Wells, Oscar Wilde, Robbie Williams, Tennessee Williams, Terry Wogan, Stevie Wonder, William Wordsworth.

SUCCESS TIPS FOR THE TIGER

In general, the Tiger should aim to become more self-disciplined and focused. While he may start a project or activity full of enthusiasm, he can abandon it completely if he sees something else which he considers more interesting. This way he does not always reap the rewards of his efforts or indeed give himself the chance to build up his expertise. When he has set himself some goal or task, the Tiger should resolve to see it through. With dedication and self-discipline, he will achieve more as well as enjoy a greater level of success.

The Tiger may be sociable, but he is independent-minded and likes to set about his activities in his own way. However, there will be many times when he could profit from talking his ideas over with those who are able to give him informed advice. He must not close his mind to the help others can give. Sometimes being too single-minded can undermine what he is hoping to achieve.

The Tiger does have a rebellious streak to his nature and there will be times when he will disagree with certain restrictions and rules placed upon him. However, in certain instances, he may find it in his interests to acquiesce rather than pit himself so firmly against others. Particularly in his earlier years, to rebel frequently will do him no favours. This can sometimes be a bitter pill for the self-willed Tiger to swallow, but he must be aware that without care and respect towards others, he may not always make the best of himself or show himself in the most favourable light.

The Tiger likes to live life at a fast pace and can be hasty and impulsive. While he may be eager to get results, too much haste can sometimes lead to errors. The Tiger would do better to plan ahead and consider the implications of his actions. Haste, impulsiveness and recklessness can cost him dear and again prevent him from achieving all he might.

One of the Tiger's greatest strengths is his ability to think creatively. He has an inventive mind and he owes it to himself to nurture, develop and promote his ideas and talents. Admittedly, sometimes his efforts may not quite work out, but the Tiger should persist and have faith in himself. His contribution *can* make a difference and sometimes lead him to great success. Indeed, it has often been said that all it takes to succeed is just one good idea. The Tiger is capable of generating many – and he owes it to himself to use them to good effect.

SOME FINAL THOUGHTS FROM TIGERS

Most roads lead men homewards,
My road leads me forth.
John Masefield

You cannot dream yourself into a character, you must hammer
and forge one for yourself.
James A. Froude

Nothing great will ever be achieved without great men, and men
are great only if they are deemed to be so.
Charles de Gaulle

Every man of action has a strong dose of egotism, pride,
hardness and cunning.
Charles de Gaulle

I'm sure you have a theme: the theme of life. You can embellish
it or desecrate it, but it's your theme, and as long as you follow
it, you will experience harmony and peace of mind.
Agatha Christie

Not knowing when the dawn will come, I open every door.
Emily Dickinson

The mere sense of living is joy enough.
Emily Dickinson

Make voyages. Attempt them. There's nothing else.
Tennessee Williams

The true perfection of man lies not in what man has, but in what man is.

Oscar Wilde

The aim of life is self-development, to realize one's nature perfectly.

Oscar Wilde

Success is a science. If you have the conditions, you get the result.

Oscar Wilde

The
Rabbit

Whether scurrying around lush green fields or living quietly as a domestic pet, there is an air of serenity about the Rabbit. Provided there is no obvious threat, he will be generally content with his lot. The Rabbit seeks a secure and settled lifestyle, and so it is with those born under the fourth of the Chinese signs.

Quiet, calm and good-natured, the Rabbit enjoys the finer things in life. He has style, finesse and charm. He also has a good brain and a talent for reading both people and situations. If he senses problems or dangers looming, he will do all he can to either defuse them or get out of the way. Sometimes, in order to preserve the peace, he may even turn a blind eye to what is going on. The Rabbit hates arguments, tension and stressful situations. To some, he may appear cool and aloof. This is his way of avoiding situations or people he feels could bring him problems. He is all for a calm and peaceable existence.

However, this desire, commendable though it is, can some-times prevent the Rabbit from achieving all that he might. His reticence and his dislike of change and of the cut and thrust of some business situations mean that he does not always promote himself as much as he could. He may be skilled and astute, but he may not have the drive and steely ambition of some. It is for this reason that when choosing a career, the Rabbit should aim for one which will allow him to develop in his own way rather than place him in too aggressive or pressurized an environment.

The Rabbit also likes to feel in control of his situation, so again he may not always put himself forward for fear of the consequences that could result. He dislikes the unknown and will sometimes feel it is better to remain in a situation he knows well and can handle rather than jeopardize his stability by venturing forth. However, in order to progress it is sometimes necessary to take risks, and to realize potential it is necessary to take action. To make the most of his talents, the Rabbit does owe it to himself to be bolder. He has a lot in his favour, but his reticence can restrict the amount he actually achieves.

The Rabbit is, though, well respected. He enjoys being with others and has a friendly manner. He enjoys conversation and is able to remember details about others which can greatly impress. Also, as he is well read and likes to keep himself informed, he is able to hold forth on a great range of subjects. The Rabbit can be very agreeable company and he especially enjoys chatting with his many friends and either entertaining them at home (the Rabbit makes a superb host) or going out socializing.

In keeping with his careful and well-ordered manner, the Rabbit pays a great deal of attention to his appearance. Both male and female dress well, often choosing good-quality clothes that suit them. The female Rabbit takes particular care with her hair and will spend much time and money getting it as she likes it. In addition, she enjoys adding fine touches to clothes, especially in the form of jewellery. The Rabbit has style and often impeccable taste.

Both male and female Rabbit have quiet and reflective natures but do enjoy company. The female in particular will have a close and well-established group of friends, enjoys conversation and can be an engaging and often witty speaker. She is able to gauge the feelings of others and vary her response accordingly. She is much admired for her sound and often shrewd advice and is blessed with good business and financial sense as well as being creative and often gifted in the arts.

The male Rabbit has a quiet and friendly manner and with his often smart looks and wide interests, knows how to impress. He is also highly observant and a good listener as well as a good judge of character. He has refined tastes and could become an expert on some aspect of the arts or on a particular interest of his. He likes security and stability and does not handle stress well. However, throughout his life, his genial and careful manner will serve him well.

The Rabbit enjoys order and routine and will devote much time and energy to making sure his home is tidy, neat, well maintained, comfortable and homely. He will ensure that the furnishings and equipment are the best he can afford and will take particular delight in adding more aesthetic items, whether *objets d'art*, paintings or antiques. Again, his superb taste will be evident and his home will be a delight.

Even though the Rabbit often has a large family and will make sure his children are always well provided for, he is not a particularly family-oriented person. He could find the frequent demands of young children both disruptive and disturbing. Neither does he like the squabbles and occasional traumas that family life can bring. Wherever possible, the Rabbit will try to remove himself from any family bickering or any awkward situations. He will love his family dearly and will be supportive, but they must fit in with his calm and ordered lifestyle.

With his companionable nature the Rabbit makes friends with ease and from adolescence onwards is likely to have a great many romances. He also possesses a strong and healthy libido. Love and passion (and, he hopes, security) are central to him. When looking for a partner, he should ideally choose someone with an affable temperament who appreciates a settled and ordered lifestyle and has cultured tastes.

As far as his personal interests are concerned, in addition to his love of socializing, the Rabbit enjoys the arts, including literature, music, films and the theatre or other live entertainment. He also likes things of beauty and will often enjoy visiting museums and galleries as well as investigating antique shops and other places which could yield hidden treasures. Many Rabbits are keen collectors, particularly of old things which possess some beauty or charm. Also, in keeping with his appreciation of the finer things in life, the Rabbit is a connoisseur of food and drink, and when funds permit he will delight in treating himself and his loved ones to a good meal somewhere.

The Rabbit certainly likes to live life well and he will strive to make it as settled and hassle-free as he can. Those born in the summer are considered the luckiest of their sign, but all Rabbits have it within them to prosper and succeed in life. The Rabbit is intelligent, perceptive (some even psychic) and able to get on well with others. If he is prepared to assert himself and make the most of his abilities, then he can certainly achieve a great deal throughout his life.

SUCCESS AND WORK

The Rabbit is intelligent, keeps himself well informed and has a good way with others. He is able to read both situations and people well. With all this in his favour, he is certainly able to achieve a good level of success, but he does possess traits which could prevent him from doing as well as he otherwise might.

In particular the Rabbit does not like change, often preferring to stick with the familiar rather than move forward. His reticence in exploring new possibilities can mean that he loses out on some opportunities. In his working life, he will definitely need to push himself forward more if he wishes to make the most of his potential, particularly in the early years. In order to make progress, some risks do need to be taken and the Rabbit *must* accept this.

Also, while no one likes to be involved in unpleasant and fraught situations, the Rabbit actively goes out of his way to avoid these. Again, his reluctance to be at the forefront of activity can tell against him and cause him to lose out to those who are more assertive. It would certainly be in the Rabbit's interests to be heard more rather than to stay behind the scenes.

Ironically, if ever the Rabbit does find himself in a position of great power, he can become quite a formidable figure, protecting his role and authority with considerable might!

The Rabbit can do particularly well in careers which allow him to use his creative talents. He can make a fine writer, journalist, musician and performer. With his eye for beauty and quality, he can also enjoy success as a designer in the world of fashion or as an antique dealer. He can also excel in positions which require detailed research and, with his eloquent style, could be attracted to the legal profession, particularly as a barrister or legal representative. Rabbits also make fine teachers and some, with their often strong faith and ability to relate effectively to others, choose to enter the Church or aim to help others through some form of counselling work.

There is certainly much that the Rabbit can succeed in, but generally he should avoid the type of work which can be disruptive to his lifestyle, for instance work which requires him to travel at short notice, is especially competitive or entails being in a frenzied environment. The Rabbit prefers working in an ordered and structured way and in an area which he will find satisfying and intellectually challenging. If he chooses well, then with his considerable ability, keen intellect and genial manner, he has it within him to impress. How much he achieves is, though, dependent upon how he promotes his talents.

SUCCESS AND MONEY

The Rabbit is good at handling money and is often able to enjoy a good standard of living as well as be materially well off.

As with most areas of his life, in money matters the Rabbit proceeds carefully. He does not like taking risks, especially when his security is at stake. Rather than be tempted into wild speculation, when investing or saving he prefers to stick with safer and more established companies or opt for schemes with a known return. Also, with his eye for quality and beauty, he may choose to put some of his money into things which he can appreciate, such as antiques. Sometimes these can become a good investment for him. The Rabbit also has an eye for a bargain and can be a shrewd buyer.

In general, the Rabbit enjoys a fine lifestyle. He will seek out the best-quality products and opt for the more expensive restaurants or the better seats at a show. When he wants to enjoy himself (or impress others) he will spend quite freely. He is, though, a good provider and will always try to ensure his loved ones have all they need. Where home finances are concerned, he likes to keep things in order and make sure his commitments are covered.

As with so much in his life, the Rabbit does like to be in control of his financial situation and if he does ever experience misfortune this will often come as the result of interference from others or from not following his own intuition. For this reason, the Rabbit should be wary of becoming involved in anything about which he has misgivings. Not only will he feel uncomfortable in himself (as again his level of security could be affected), but his instinct is often a reliable indicator of the likely outcome.

The Rabbit is, though, generally successful in money matters and, with his careful and methodical approach, looks after his finances well. While he can at times be extravagant, he will always make sure he only spends what he can afford. As with so much in his life, he does not like to leave things to chance or do anything that could undermine his secure, stable and often comfortable existence.

SUCCESS AND LOVE

Passionate, affectionate and sensual, the Rabbit enjoys being in love and the happiness and indeed security a steady and meaningful relationship can bring.

With his quiet and companionable nature, the Rabbit will certainly have no problem attracting admirers and is likely to enjoy many romances before he settles down. When in love and aware of the devotion of another, the Rabbit will be blissfully happy, although should the relationship flounder, he will detest any unpleasantness and wrangling that may occur, wishing that life and love would run smoothly and without so many complications. However, while the course of true love will sometimes be painful, the Rabbit is resilient. He needs someone and will, sooner or later, find someone.

Love for the Rabbit can be an intoxicating experience and in his early adult life he can sometimes be quite promiscuous. However, in his quest for a partner, he will find most happiness with those who appreciate an ordered and settled lifestyle. The Rabbit does not like turmoil or being forever active. Instead, he wants to share, to appreciate and enjoy the finer things in life and he desires security. With a partner who is supportive, has similar values and tastes and is considerate of the Rabbit's sensitive nature, he can find great happiness.

SUCCESS WITH OTHERS

The Rabbit has a great way with others and makes a good friend. People feel at ease in his company and he often has much of interest and value to say. While there will be some signs he will feel more at ease with than others, his relations with most will be sound.

With a Rat

Although the Rat has qualities that the Rabbit admires, in general he is too active and brash for the Rabbit's liking and their temperaments will clash. Relations between them will be variable but rarely close.

In the parent–child relationship, the Rabbit parent will admire the young Rat's keen and resourceful nature and quickness to learn. However, the young Rat is often lively and boisterous and could become quite a handful for the more placid Rabbit.

As colleagues, their different strengths can often prove complementary, with the Rabbit particularly valuing the Rat's resourcefulness, enterprise and drive. Admittedly they may not care for each other, but if they can keep their relationship strictly professional and work in harmony towards specific objectives, then these two can achieve a fair degree of success.

In love, the Rat and Rabbit are particularly passionate and sensual signs and both attach a great deal of importance to their home and social life. However, the Rabbit desires a peaceful existence and could find the bustling energy and vitality of the Rat difficult to bear. Also the Rat's candid nature can unnerve the sensitive Rabbit. If their relationship is to endure, much understanding and consideration will be required.

With an Ox

With their often similar outlooks and values, the Rabbit gets on well with the Ox.

In the parent—child relationship, the Rabbit parent will help the young Ox to develop well, providing the right level of encouragement as well as being understanding of the young Ox's often quiet and reflective nature. As parent and child they have much in common and there will be a close bond between them.

As colleagues, the Rabbit and Ox work well together. Both enjoy order and method and they will also benefit from each other's strengths. The Rabbit will particularly appreciate the Ox's confident and resolute approach. Neither enjoys taking risks or diverting from more conventional procedures and together they can achieve a great deal.

In love, the Rabbit and Ox are well suited. With their similar interests and tastes, they will understand and support each other well. The Rabbit will value having such a dependable and supportive partner. Together they will pour much energy into their home and aim to lead a quiet, settled and very content lifestyle. A great match.

With a Tiger

The Rabbit thinks well of the sincere and sociable Tiger and the two signs can learn much from each other. Relations between them will often be good.

In the parent–child relationship, the Rabbit parent will do much to support the young Tiger's keen and inquisitive nature, and particularly guide him academically. He may sometimes despair of the Tiger child's high and self-willed spirit, but they will mean much to each other and will come to accept and accommodate their different natures.

As colleagues, these two signs recognize each other's individual strengths and will combine them to good effect. The Rabbit will appreciate the Tiger's creative flair and enterprise and at the same time temper his more impulsive and reckless notions. When united in a common purpose these two can, by virtue of their different talents, make a successful team.

In love, again these two complement each other. The Rabbit will draw strength from the Tiger's confident and ebullient nature and as both are keen socializers, they will often enjoy an active social life. They will, though, need to be respectful of each other's natures and the Rabbit must allow the Tiger a certain independence rather than expect complete togetherness. But their respect and love for each other will be strong and they can make a happy match.

With another Rabbit

With similar values and outlooks, two Rabbits will greatly enjoy each other's company and will get on splendidly.

In the parent–child relationship, the Rabbit parent will understand the sensitivities of a young Rabbit and will do much to support and encourage the child. The young Rabbit will thrive in his care and appreciate the secure atmosphere found in a Rabbit home. There will be a great bond between them.

As colleagues, their considerable business skills and fine judgement will serve them well. There will be a good level of trust between them and any venture they set up will be efficient, well managed and often successful. They make a good level-headed team.

In love, bliss and happiness. Both desire a settled and stable home life and this is what they will aim to create. Supportive and understanding of each other and with many interests they can share, two Rabbits make an excellent match.

With a Dragon

The Rabbit likes the breezy and confident style of the Dragon and finds him inspirational company. There is considerable respect between the two signs.

In the parent–child relationship, the Rabbit parent will be proud of the young Dragon's keen and enterprising nature and will encourage him well. There will be a good understanding between them, although the Rabbit parent will sometimes wish the young Dragon was of a quieter and more compliant disposition!

As colleagues, these two signs respect each other's strengths and can make a successful team. The Rabbit will particularly value the Dragon's enthusiastic and determined approach, and by combining their talents and ideas, they can achieve a great deal.

In love, there is often considerable attraction. Passionate, sensual and caring, the Rabbit and Dragon can mean much to each other and the Rabbit will appreciate having such a confident and resourceful partner. There *will* be differences they will need to address, particularly as the Dragon prefers to lead a more active lifestyle than the Rabbit, but if they can adjust to each other and show some understanding, these two can make a strong match.

‿ With a Snake

The Rabbit appreciates the refined and thoughtful ways of the Snake and relations between them are good.

In the parent–child relationship, the Rabbit parent will relate well to the often quiet and reflective Snake child. They understand each other well and there will be much love between them.

As colleagues, they possess skills and ideas, but sometimes could lack the drive to realize their potential. There could be much deliberation and planning, but they could do with someone else to spur them into action.

In love, these two can find much happiness. Both enjoy a quiet and settled lifestyle, and as both have cultured tastes, they will have many interests they can share. They will be very supportive of each other and the Rabbit will delight in having such a thoughtful and generally calm partner. A successful match.

‿ With a Horse

The Rabbit is keenly aware of the Horse's volatile and restless nature and will not feel at ease in his company. Relations between the two signs will be tricky.

In the parent–child relationship, the Rabbit parent will find the independent-minded and often lively young Horse quite a handful. Although both will be keen to work out their differences and understand each other better, relations will at times be awkward.

As colleagues, their different styles and outlooks will cause problems. The Rabbit will find the Horse impulsive and hasty and will prefer a more cautious and planned approach. These two do not work well together.

In love, again there will be many differences. There may be a strong physical attraction and both are very passionate signs, but the Rabbit prefers a quieter lifestyle than that of the restless Horse. The Horse also has a tendency to speak his mind and a short temper, and this can trouble the sensitive Rabbit. This will be a challenging match.

With a Goat

The Rabbit has a great fondness for the easy-going Goat and the two signs get on very well indeed.

In the parent–child relationship, the young Goat will respond well to be a calm and supportive influence of a Rabbit parent. There will be a close and loving bond between them, made all the stronger by their similar interests.

As colleagues, the Rabbit and Goat will like and trust each other and if their work is in any way creative, they can achieve great success. These two will often inspire and bring out the best in each other.

In love, they are well suited, particularly as both seek a calm, harmonious and settled existence. Also, with their artistic and creative leanings, they will have many interests in common as well as an appreciation of the finer things in life. The Rabbit will value the Goat's sincere and affectionate nature as well as enjoy the security of having such an understanding and supportive partner. Provided they manage to avoid too many problems, as neither copes well with stress, theirs can be a close and successful match.

With a Monkey

The Rabbit likes the cheerful and positive spirit of the Monkey and on a personal level relations between the two signs are reasonably good.

In the parent–child relationship, the Rabbit parent will find the sometimes mischievous and lively young Monkey a disruptive influence on his calm and well-ordered existence. However, despite the occasional clash, these two will develop respect for each other as well as share some common interests. Relations will get better as the Monkey matures.

As colleagues, their different approaches will cause difficulty. The Rabbit prefers to plan ahead and stick to tried and tested methods, while the Monkey is more elastic in the tactics he uses, sometimes being artful or very crafty. This does not sit well with the Rabbit and in work situations there will be a general lack of understanding between the two signs. Not a successful combination.

In love, they will appreciate each other's qualities more. In particular the Rabbit will enjoy the Monkey's warm, outgoing and generally optimistic nature. They will have many different interests they can share and can form a close and meaningful relationship. A good match.

With a Rooster

The Rooster is too abrupt and matter of fact for the Rabbit and relations between the two signs will be poor.

In the parent–child relationship, the Rabbit parent will admire the young Rooster's keen and alert manner and quickness to learn, but could have difficulty in coping with his self-willed and independent nature. Relations will sometimes be awkward.

As colleagues, again their temperaments are not suited. Both may be methodical and work hard, but the Rabbit will not be comfortable with the Rooster's often demanding attitude. The Rooster likes to organize and be in control and their different approaches will often conflict.

In love, again this can prove a difficult match. Although the Rabbit may admire the Rooster's sincere, well-meaning and orderly ways, the Rooster likes to keep active and to speak his mind, while the Rabbit prefers a much more settled existence and could often feel hurt by the Rooster's forthright manner. Both signs possess many fine qualities, but they are not well suited.

With a Dog

The Rabbit likes and trusts the noble Dog and relations between the two signs are good.

In the parent–child relationship, the young and dutiful Dog will feel at ease with his good-natured Rabbit parent and strive to please. The Rabbit will do much to help lift the young Dog's spirits whenever he feels down or is lacking in confidence. There will be a close and loving bond between them.

As colleagues, the Rabbit and Dog can fare well. Both are conscientious and thorough and have good business sense. By combining their skills they can make a successful team, although if they ever suffer a reversal, problems can occur, as neither copes well with anxiety or stress.

In love, theirs can be a successful match, particularly as both seek a stable and secure existence. They will enjoy a good rapport and will be supportive of each other as well as share many interests. The Rabbit will particularly value the loyal, dependable and caring ways of the Dog. These two can find much contentment together.

With a Pig

The Rabbit gets on well with the friendly and easy-going Pig and there is a good understanding between the two signs.

In the parent–child relationship, there will be great love and affection between the Rabbit parent and Pig child. The young Pig will respond well to Rabbit's calm and genial manner and will work hard to please, while the Rabbit will enjoy the young Pig's joyful and inquisitive ways. There will be a close bond between them.

As colleagues, relations will again be good. Both signs have sound business sense and with their astute natures and eagerness to build a secure future, they will work well together and can achieve a great deal. The Rabbit will be particularly glad to have such a robust and enterprising colleague that he can depend upon.

In love, the Rabbit and Pig make a happy match. Both are peace-loving signs who appreciate the finer things in life and with their similar interests and outlooks, they can build a strong relationship. They also respect each other's feelings and will do much to support one another, which is something the Rabbit will especially appreciate. As a couple they are well suited.

SUCCESS THROUGH LIFE

While some Chinese signs have differing fortunes during the various stages of their lives, this is not so with the Rabbit. With his generally quiet and peaceable manner, he can find contentment throughout his life *provided* the situation around him is relatively stable. If this is lacking and he feels insecure, then his life can become difficult, especially on an emotional level. The Rabbit does not cope well with stress or sudden change.

As a child, the Rabbit is usually content and if he is in a secure home environment, he will thrive. He is a keen learner and will aim to please both those at home and at school. He is careful, thorough and imaginative. However, he is also sensitive, often taking criticism very much to heart. Should he ever be subjected to any form of bullying, he will feel it deeply. If the young Rabbit is ever worried over a particular matter, he should be prepared to talk his concerns over with others. Throughout his life, the Rabbit will find much value and reassurance in being forthcoming rather than brooding over his concerns by himself.

As he matures, the Rabbit will continue to do well academically, often enjoying the challenges offered by more advanced work. He will also enjoy himself, with plenty of socializing, partying and romance.

With his often good qualifications and fine abilities, including his judgement and ability to get on well with others, the Rabbit will impress others as he enters his chosen career. In an ideal world, he would develop in his own time and way, but, with so many organizations being subject to change, he *will* have to learn to adjust to the situations in which he finds himself. Rather than live in fear of change, the Rabbit should view it as something that is inevitable and that can often give rise to new opportunities. At times he should be more adventurous in his attitude. He would reap more rewards as a result, as well as make greater progress.

However, as the Rabbit develops his skills and grows in confidence, he will find that his abilities and skills will propel him forward and over time enable him to rise to positions of seniority and responsibility.

In all his activities, the Rabbit will value the support of his partner and loved ones. They are his prop and should this ever be missing, the Rabbit could find life more difficult. Many Rabbits tend to have large families, although the Rabbit could sometimes find the disruptive and demanding nature of young children tricky to cope with. However, as his children get older, his relations with them can become an especially valuable part of his life. Family-wise, middle age can be a smoother and more meaningful time for the Rabbit. As Frank Lloyd Wright, a Rabbit, once noted, 'The longer I live, the more beautiful life becomes.'

As the Rabbit passes into older age he will often be comfortably well off and content with his interests and with spending time with those around him. As always, his family and social circle will be important to him. The Rabbit often lives to an advanced age but some, unfortunately, find the later years can sometimes be lonelier than they would wish.

Although life will throw up its challenges and obstacles, provided there are not too many of them and the Rabbit feels comfortable with his situation, he will prosper and be very content.

FAMOUS RABBITS

Bertie Ahern, Drew Barrymore, David Beckham, Harry Belafonte, Ingrid Bergman, St Bernadette, Melanie Brown, Emma Bunton, James Caan, Nicolas Cage, Thomas Carlyle, Lewis Carroll, Fidel Castro, John Cleese, Confucius, Marie Curie, Johnny Depp, Albert Einstein, George Eliot, W. C. Fields, Bridget Fonda, James Fox, Sir David Frost, James Galway, Cary Grant, Edvard Grieg, Oliver Hardy, Seamus Heaney, Bob Hope, Whitney Houston, John Howard, John Hurt, Anjelica Huston, Chrissie Hynde, Henry James, David Jason, Michael Jordan, Michael Keaton, John Keats, Judith Krantz, Danny La Rue, Cheryl Ladd, Gina Lollobrigida, Henry Wadsworth Longfellow, Ali MacGraw, George Michael, Roger Moore, Mike Myers, Brigitte Nielsen, George Orwell, John Peel, Edith Piaf, Sidney Poitier, John Ruskin, Mort Sahl, Elisabeth Schwarzkopf, Neil Sedaka, Jane Seymour, Frank Sinatra, Fatboy Slim, Sting, J. R. R. Tolkien, Tina Turner, Luther Vandross, Queen Victoria, Orson Welles, Walt Whitman, Robin Williams, Kate Winslet, Tiger Woods, Frank Lloyd Wright.

SUCCESS TIPS FOR THE RABBIT

Success is a journey. It is a case of venturing forth and making the most of ideas and inborn talents. However, the Rabbit sometimes denies himself the chance to reap his full rewards for fear of change. He is a great one for living in the comfort zone! However, in order to progress and maximize potential, it *is* necessary to move forward. Failure to do so could leave many Rabbits falling into a rut and underachieving. While the road to success is not an easy one and sometimes there will be times of disappointment, by putting himself forward the Rabbit will stand to gain more and will feel more fulfilled as well as have a better chance of realizing his rich potential.

Although the Rabbit has a friendly and amiable nature, he can at times appear cool, aloof and even superficial. Often the reason for this is that his 'defence mechanisms' are up and he is avoiding situations about which he has misgivings. Rather than let his body language and manner speak for him, it could be in his interests to be more open in expressing his views. Caginess or aloofness will sometimes lower him in the eyes of others, while if he were prepared to be more open, he would often strengthen the respect others have for him. Again, the Rabbit's reticence can be to his detriment and he should aim to be more forthcoming. It is better for him to win respect by being open than to lose it by indifference.

Although the Rabbit sets about his various activities in an organized manner, it could also be in his interests to set himself some specific goals. These can be personal, professional or financial, but whatever targets the Rabbit sets, he will find they can help propel him forward. It would be useful for him to consider one-year and three-year goals and, once he has decided upon them, to write them down.

Also, the Rabbit should always maintain interests outside his usual work. These can provide an ideal escape for him as well as sometimes be another outlet for his talents. His interests can also help him help keep his life in balance and for the Rabbit, who so likes to remain on an even keel, this is vital. At stressful times, the Rabbit could find that in addition to immersing himself in his interests, some suitable light exercises such as those found in yoga and *tai chi* could help him relax and be more at one with himself.

At times in his life the Rabbit will find himself in a dilemma and, when much is at stake, he can be prone to indecision. However, he has one factor in his favour and throughout his life he should make the most of it: the Rabbit is highly intuitive. Some are even psychic. Accordingly, when making decisions, the Rabbit should rely on his innermost feelings. So often they will be a reliable indicator of the path he should follow. He should trust himself, for the Rabbit is his own best friend.

SOME FINAL THOUGHTS FROM RABBITS

Let every dawn of the morning be to you as the beginning of life. And let every setting of the sun be to you as its close. Then let every one of these short lives leave its sure record of some kindly thing done for others, some good strength or knowledge gained for yourself.
John Ruskin

I know the price of success; dedication, hard work, and an unremitting devotion to the things you want to see happen.
Frank Lloyd Wright

The thing always happens that you really believe in; and the belief in a thing makes it happen.
Frank Lloyd Wright

Wondrous is the strength of cheerfulness, and its power or endurance – the cheerful man will do more in the same time, will do it better, will persevere in it longer than the sad or sullen.
Thomas Carlyle

There is no man, no woman, so small but that they cannot make their life great by high endeavour.
Thomas Carlyle

The talent of success is nothing more than doing what you can well and doing well whatever you do, without a thought of fame.
Henry Wadsworth Longfellow

It seems to me we can never give up longing and wishing while we are thoroughly alive. There are certain things we feel to be beautiful and good, and we much hunger after them.
George Eliot

Our deeds determine us, as much as we determine our deeds.
George Eliot

It's never too late to be what you might have been.
George Eliot

The
Dragon

Colourful, vibrant and so full of energy, the Dragon has danced at the head of many a procession. He likes to be noticed as well as exercise his charm. And this holds true for so many born under the fifth Chinese sign.

Dragons are active, assertive and have a great way with others. They know how to impress and with their flamboyance and zest, they like to be at the forefront of much that goes on. The Dragon may be the only legendary creature in Chinese astrology but it does not stop him from weaving his magic on others as well as bringing with him the four great blessings of the East: wealth, virtue, harmony and long life. It is indeed fortunate to have a Dragon living under one's roof, especially as he is born under the sign of luck.

One of the main features of the Dragon is the faith that he has in himself. He knows that he is capable of achieving a great deal and that by applying himself he can realize his ambitions. He possesses a very strong will and once he has set himself a target, he will do his utmost to reach it. He is bold, forceful and can at times be daring. He likes action and is never one to sit on the fence or wait for chances to present themselves. Instead he goes out and looks for them. As George Bernard Shaw, himself a Dragon, once declared, 'The people who get on in this world are the people who get up and look for the circumstances they want, and, if they can't find them, make them.'

The Dragon is scrupulous in his dealings with others. He is honest and trustworthy, speaks truthfully and to the point and expects others to do likewise. He has a particular disdain of hypocrisy and falseness, although sometimes his trust is misplaced and he does leave himself vulnerable to those less honourable than himself.

The Dragon likes to keep himself occupied and nearly always has some projects to do or aims to reach. He thrives on challenge and should he ever find himself thwarted or with nothing to do, he will soon find something else. The Dragon seems to have boundless energy, an insatiable curiosity and a desire to keep active. Also he has high standards and is certainly not forgiving of poor excuses, half-hearted efforts or shoddy workmanship.

The Dragon's drive, commitment and self-belief will take him far during his life and he can look forward to being fortunate in many of his endeavours. However, he does have his faults which, if not watched, can tell against him. Sometimes his eagerness to get results makes him impatient and causes him to overlook details or to commit himself to activities without realizing the full implications. He is also very demanding of others and when those around him do not meet his standards, he will certainly tell them so. He can be direct and forthright in expressing his views and while some may appreciate his candour, others can be upset by his bluntness. Sometimes more consideration, both in the actions he is about to take and the way he passes comment, would not go amiss.

The Dragon is also very much his own master and while he will quite happily dispense advice, he will rarely seek it. In some activities he can be particularly independent-minded and, as a consequence, can sometimes miss out on help that he could benefit from. The Dragon would always do well to be more open and receptive to the advice of those around him.

However, while the Dragon does, like all signs, have his faults, his sincerity, enthusiasm and commitment will often bring him considerable success. In his work, he will delight in meeting challenges and reaching (and often surpassing) the targets he and others have set. However, he does need a challenge to be at his best and if this is ever lacking or he feels uninspired, he can quickly become bored. He dislikes the mundane. It is for this reason that the Dragon likes to be involved in what is going on rather than be on the sidelines. He enjoys being a key player, even though he is an individualist and likes to retain a certain level of independence in what he does.

This also filters through to the Dragon's personal life. While he enjoys company and will have many friends, there are quite a few Dragons who opt to remain single rather than marry or have a permanent partner, as they are not prepared to compromise their way of life for another. This applies both to male and female. While neither will ever be short of admirers, they will remain very much in charge of their situation.

Both male and female are direct and straightforward in their manner, as well as keen to make the most of their talents. The female Dragon in particular involves herself in a multitude of different activities as well as maintaining a good social life. While many years ago it was said that a woman's place was in the home, this rarely applied to the female Dragon. Neither the male nor female will ever allow themselves to get cooped up in their home. Although they will keep it well maintained and efficiently run, they favour activity and will often be busy with a variety of projects and interests rather than sitting too long with their feet up. The Dragon is never one for a routine or mundane existence!

In appearance, both the male and female tend to opt for smart but practical clothes, with the female preferring a plain style rather than embellishing her clothes or herself with lots of jewellery or make up. Instead she simply lets her personality shine through, usually most effectively.

While some Dragons choose to remain single, many do marry and often quite young. However, as the Dragon can be demanding and is not one for living too regimented a lifestyle, he should make sure his partner shares his outlook and has similar interests to his own. The Dragon can make a loyal and caring companion, but he does like to hold sway!

If he becomes a parent, the Dragon will be very supportive of his children, but he will have high expectations. Most children will benefit from his kind and firm guidance, though, and, as the Dragon's life is invariably rich and interesting, his children's lives will also often be full of wonder and excitement.

As far as the Dragon's personal interests are concerned, he is often a keen traveller and very much enjoys discovering new areas. He does possess an adventurous streak and particularly likes venturing off the usual tourist map. He also likes to lead an active social life and as he possesses such a keen and inventive mind, he will rarely find himself short of other interests, although often these will be of a passing rather than permanent nature. The Dragon is usually keen to try something out, master the challenge it offers and then move on to something else. Life for him is a continuous voyage of discovery.

As the Dragon is so keen on action and sets about his activities with such sense and purpose, his life will be eventful and often successful. It is considered less fortunate if he is born during a storm, but all Dragons have the drive, the personality and so often the luck to secure what they want in life.

SUCCESS AND WORK

One of the greatest differences between those who succeed in their work and those who drift or remain mediocre is enthusiasm. Enthusiasm lifts performance. It motivates and inspires *and* it brings results. And the Dragon is invariably enthusiastic. He likes to give of his best, to use his skills and ideas and to produce good work. He cares about what he does and this, together with his high standards, often enables him to rise to the top of his profession. The Dragon is an achiever who leads by example.

The Dragon also enjoys challenge. He likes to test himself and is forever learning. There is a Chinese proverb which states: 'Without experience one gains no wisdom.' In his working life, the Dragon is forever experiencing and then putting his experience to good use.

In his business dealings the Dragon is honest and straightforward and this, combined with his commitment, enables him to win the confidence of others. They know what to expect of him, are prepared to put their faith in him and are rarely disappointed.

However, by setting himself high standards and being something of a perfectionist, the Dragon can be demanding of those around him, expecting them to follow his example. Those who do not share his commitment or standards will soon fall foul of him and he can be blunt and forthright in his manner. This can sometimes cause problems with colleagues. The Dragon is prepared to accept this, however, if it achieves the results and standards he seeks. His style may not always win him friends, but it can be effective.

However, while the Dragon is often successful in his chosen career, he can sometimes risk everything by being too hasty or impulsive. In his desire to achieve, he sometimes acts without thinking the consequences through or ignores details which could in time prove important. More planning would not go amiss. Also, the Dragon should be prepared to listen to advice. He can be so set on a course of action that he remains blind to what others are telling him. It would be in his own interests to take the time to listen to the views of those around him and then to consider them.

As he is so versatile, the Dragon can achieve success in many different types of work. However, because he does tend to get bored easily and hates being in too much of a routine, he should aim for positions which offer variety and challenge. He needs to use his initiative and to be active. Among the many positions that could suit the Dragon are those that enable him to meet others, such as marketing, retailing and PR work. Also, as he enjoys being in the limelight, he can make an effective spokesperson or politician or achieve success in the media or show business. He does have the drive and often the charisma that can set him apart from others.

With his ability to lead by example, the Dragon can also do well in the armed services, in a managerial position or in running his own business. His ability to solve problems and think creatively can also make him an effective inventor or developer and, with the opportunities and challenges in the computer industry, some Dragons could find themselves particularly adept in software development or in some form of computer support.

For those Dragons who are more sportingly inclined, this is another area in which they can often excel professionally, especially with their strong competitive instinct. The Dragon can make a particularly inspirational captain.

It has often been said that the harder you work, the luckier you get. This certainly applies to the Dragon. Because of his industry and commitment, opportunities will often come his way. With his enterprise, enthusiasm and the faith he has in his abilities, he has it within him to both achieve *and* succeed. And, as with so much in his life, in his work he will also enjoy a good measure of luck.

SUCCESS AND MONEY

The Dragon will rarely find himself wanting for money. He has the resourcefulness and ability to earn a good income and can certainly be well off in his middle and later years.

However, while the Dragon can earn a lot, he can spend a lot too. He is generous towards his family and friends and enjoys buying himself treats. Indeed, to him, money is the reward for his hard work and is there to be enjoyed. But while the Dragon can sometimes spend rather too readily, he does keep a watch over his financial position and should he ever find himself in deficit or owing money, he will work increasingly hard to rectify the position.

As with other areas in his life, the Dragon is scrupulous in his financial undertakings. However, his trust in others can sometimes be misplaced and he can show himself naïve and vulnerable. Should he ever have a nagging doubt over any financial undertaking or scheme he is about to enter into, he should take the time to seek clarification rather than take risks or believe all he is told.

Also, while the Dragon does so like to enjoy his money, sometimes more forethought could be to his advantage. By at least taking more time over his purchases and looking closely at the choices available, he could end up with better products as well as save himself unnecessary outlay. Again, impulsiveness can cost the Dragon dear. Also, when he does find himself with surplus funds, rather than be so tempted to spend, it could be in his interests to set a certain amount aside for his future, perhaps in a savings scheme. If he adds to this on a regular basis, it can not only grow into a useful asset, but also be a financial cushion should the need ever arise.

However, with his skills, enterprise and considerable earning ability, the Dragon is usually able to support the good standard of living that he seeks and to be comfortably off in his later life.

SUCCESS AND LOVE

The Dragon is great fun to be with. He enjoys life and with his warm, friendly and lively manner he makes popular company and can win the hearts of many. He will rarely be short of admirers, is passionate and sensual, and usually has a strong libido.

The Dragon often chooses to marry young, but while this can sometimes prove to be lasting and happy, he should still be wary of embarking on marriage at too early an age. It is better to get to know a prospective partner really well and build a solid foundation to the relationship rather than discover – perhaps too late – that there are many differences that need to be reconciled. Also, there are some Dragons who regard marriage as a way to break free from parental control and if it is this rather than true love that drives the Dragon, then the relationship could in time also flounder. When considering settling down with someone, the Dragon should not be too hasty.

As a partner, the Dragon would do well to choose someone who has a similarly adventurous outlook, appreciates and maintains the high standards he seeks (remembering the Dragon can be quite demanding!) and allows him to pursue his own interests. After all, the Dragon is not one for too restrictive a lifestyle. He will himself enjoy living with someone who has wide interests and is an intellectual match for him.

While many Dragons do settle down successfully with a partner, there are some who prefer to remain single. While these will enjoy the companionship of the opposite sex and will often have many romances, their freedom and independent lifestyle are just too precious to lose.

SUCCESS WITH OTHERS

Being the showman that he is, the Dragon does like an audience. He is outgoing and sociable and makes interesting company, although his direct and sometimes domineering style does not suit everyone. He will certainly find there are some Chinese signs he gets on with far better than others.

With a Rat

The Dragon greatly admires the Rat's lively and resourceful spirit and relations between the two signs are often excellent.

In the parent–child relationship, the Dragon parent will admire the young Rat's keen and resourceful ways and will provide just the right level of encouragement and discipline for the young Rat to thrive. There will be a close and loving bond between them.

As colleagues, the Rat and Dragon make a successful combination. Both are enterprising, ambitious and full of ideas. They work well together, with the Dragon especially appreciating the Rat's business sense and ability to identify opportunities. These two will spur each other on and could go far.

In love, the Rat and Dragon can find much happiness. These two live life to the full and, with their lively natures and multitude of interests, are well suited. The Dragon will be particularly taken with the Rat's effervescent and companionable nature as well as his wonderful charm. These two will love each other dearly and can make an excellent match.

With an Ox

The Dragon may respect the solid and steadfast nature of the Ox, but because of the different ways in which they conduct themselves, these two rarely become close friends or associates.

In the parent–child relationship, the Dragon parent could have some difficulty in coming to terms with the Ox child's quiet and sometimes solitary ways and may feel the Ox child should be more outgoing and adventurous in his outlook. While he means well and will do much to encourage the young Ox, the rapport between them may not always be that satisfactory.

As colleagues, both maintain high standards and are keen to give their best. Both also like to do things their own way and can be forthright and resolute. However, if they can join together in a common objective and combine their individual strengths, then with the Ox's tenacity and Dragon's enterprise, these two could achieve a great deal.

In love, the Dragon will admire the sincerity and the calm, methodical ways of the Ox. For a time, as each explores the different world and outlook of the other, relations can be good, but the longer term prospects will be more difficult. The Dragon prefers a much more energetic lifestyle to the Ox and as both are so strong-willed and forthright, this can prove a tricky match.

With a Tiger

The Dragon enjoys the company of the bold, energetic and exciting Tiger and the two signs generally get on well.

In the parent–child relationship, the Dragon parent will delight in the young Tiger's keen and spirited nature and guide him well. Admittedly the young Tiger's rebellious and sometimes obstinate tendencies will lead to the inevitable clash, but there will be a great bond between parent and child.

As colleagues, anything is possible. These two thrive on action and together their ideas, enterprise and enthusiasm can lead them far. Each will encourage the other and, provided they do not overreach themselves or take one risk too many, they can achieve a great level of success.

In love, there will be passion, excitement and so much to share. Life for these two can be a wonderful and exhilarating experience, with the Dragon admiring the Tiger's lively and generous spirit as well as his warm and affectionate nature. However, both can be restless and impulsive and require the freedom to pursue their individual interests. If they can accommodate their differences, then theirs can be a successful and exciting match.

With a Rabbit

Although these signs may have their differences in style and outlook, the Dragon admires and respects the Rabbit and relations between them will be good.

In the parent–child relationship, the Dragon parent will do much to support and encourage the Rabbit child and build up his confidence. Admittedly the young Rabbit may prefer a more settled existence than that found in a Dragon household and may feel some of the Dragon's more forthright comments deeply, but there will be a good rapport between them.

As colleagues, both are conscientious and maintain high standards and each will benefit from the other's strengths. In particular, the Dragon will appreciate the Rabbit's ability to plan and organize and will find him a wise and astute partner. By joining forces they can make an effective team.

In love, with their passionate natures, there can be a strong attraction between these two, with the Dragon valuing the quiet, confident and affectionate ways of the Rabbit. However, they will have their differences to reconcile. The Dragon prefers a more active lifestyle and his forthright nature can be unnerving for the more sensitive Rabbit. If both show consideration, though, it is possible for them to find much happiness together.

⟨ With another Dragon

The Dragon will greatly enjoy the company of another lively and spirited Dragon and while their sometimes strong-willed natures may cause problems, they will generally get on well together.

In the parent–child relationship, there will be a good bond between Dragon parent and child. The parent will encourage the young Dragon, but at the same time allow him sufficient freedom to develop in his own way. Admittedly there will be occasions when the Dragon child's self-willed streak will lead to confrontation – and the Dragon parent will be strict and suffer no nonsense – but there will be a good rapport between them.

As colleagues, two Dragons have the drive, enterprise and ideas to take them far. If they combine their skills well and remain committed to a particular objective, then together they are capable of considerable success. But each will try to dominate and if they cannot agree upon a division of responsibilities, then the jostling for control could undermine them.

In love, there will be passion, fun and dreams of a wonderful future. With their optimistic natures, two Dragons will start out full of hope and utterly devoted to each other. Provided they can reconcile their differences of opinion and come to terms with their two dominant natures, then they can also look forward to a full and rewarding life together.

⚞ With a Snake

The Dragon has a high regard for the Snake and the chemistry between these two signs is excellent.

In the parent–child relationship, the Dragon parent will be a good influence on the quiet and reflective Snake child. He will do much to build up the young Snake's confidence as well as help him to lose some of his shy manner. There will be great love between them.

As colleagues, each will gain from the other. The Dragon will value the Snake's often shrewd judgement as well as regard him as a useful check on his sometimes hasty and impulsive approach. They will respect each other and by combining their talents, they can achieve considerable success.

In love, these two can find great happiness, with the Dragon being especially attracted by the Snake's quiet and affectionate manner as well as enjoying his often gentle humour and thoughtful ways. Although the Dragon will prefer a more active lifestyle to the Snake and the Snake will have a tendency to be possessive, these will prove small hurdles in what can be a truly successful love match.

⚞ With a Horse

The Dragon enjoys the lively and spirited ways of the Horse and relations between these two signs will generally be good.

In the parent–child relationship, the Dragon parent will admire the young Horse's keen and enterprising spirit and, being a good disciplinarian, will guide him well. The Horse child will learn much from his Dragon parent and there will be a good bond between them.

As colleagues, the Dragon and Horse have energy and enthusiasm in abundance and the Dragon will particularly appreciate the

Horse's ability to work so hard and often with such enterprise. With their drive and ambition they make an effective combination, although once they have achieved their goal, they are more than likely to go their own ways, with their independent streaks getting the better of them.

In love, the attraction between Dragon and Horse can be strong. With often similar interests and outlooks, they have much in common and the Dragon will appreciate the Horse's lively, eloquent and practical nature. Here is a sign he can trust and love. However, both are strong-willed and like to dominate as well as speak their minds. If they can make allowances for their redoubtable natures, though, these two can make an active and fulfilling life together.

With a Goat

For a time, the Dragon can get on well with the Goat, but their different styles and attitudes will eventually lead to problems.

In the parent–child relationship, the Dragon parent will do much to build the young Goat's confidence and help him to further his interests and talents. But the young Goat is sensitive and may sometimes feel uneasy with the Dragon's blunt nature as well as pressured by his high expectations. Relations will need some careful handling – and tact and delicacy is not always a Dragon strong point!

As colleagues, the Dragon will quickly assert his authority, but will appreciate the Goat's inventive and creative flair. The Dragon can often bring out the best in the Goat and when united for a specific purpose, they can make a successful team.

In love, the initial attraction between the Dragon and Goat can be great, with the Dragon enjoying the Goat's fun-loving ways, charm, style and lively spirit. Their love for each other can be intense, but for this happy state to endure, considerable allowances will have to be made. In particular, the Dragon could become exasperated by the Goat's fickleness and swings of mood as well as his sometimes lackadaisical manner. What started with such promise could, without care, degenerate into disillusionment.

⚞ With a Monkey

The Dragon enjoys the Monkey's company and relations between the two signs can be good.

In the parent–child relationship, the Dragon parent will admire the young Monkey's keen, lively and resourceful nature and the young Monkey will develop well under the Dragon's firm and loving guidance. There will be a strong bond between them.

As colleagues, these two have ideas and enterprise and by combining their skills can achieve great success. The Dragon will particularly appreciate the Monkey's often original and imaginative approach and provided the Monkey keeps everything above board (he can, after all, be wily and crafty), these two will work well together and can achieve a great deal.

In love, with so many interests in common and similar outlooks, the pair are well suited. The Dragon will find the Monkey excellent company and appreciate his *joie de vivre*. These two like to lead full, active and interesting lives and will find life together an often rich and wonderful experience. A great and usually successful match.

⚞ With a Rooster

The Dragon admires the lively, sincere and direct manner of the Rooster and these two signs get on well.

In the parent–child relationship, relations may, though, not always be easy, with the Dragon parent at times losing patience with the sometimes demanding and pernickety Rooster child. Both are strong-willed and the Dragon is a disciplinarian, so there will inevitably be clashes. Relations will improve as the Rooster matures.

As colleagues, each values the honest and matter-of-fact nature of the other, with the Dragon especially appreciating the Rooster's efficient and well-organized approach. Together they make a fine team.

In love, these two mean much to each other. They enjoy an active lifestyle, are keen socializers and value each other's individual strengths. The Rooster will inject order into the Dragon's life and help him to channel his energies in a more focused and successful way. These two can be good for each other and can form a close and caring relationship.

With a Dog

With different outlooks and attitudes, the Dragon and Dog do not get on well.

In the parent–child relationship, the Dragon parent and Dog child may try to build up rapport and understanding, but it will not be easy. The Dragon parent's bold and direct nature does not sit comfortably with the young Dog, who responds better to a quieter approach and someone who is prepared to listen more. As a result, relations will rarely be that close.

As colleagues, again trust and accord will be lacking. Both will try to dominate and with their often different approaches, disagreements will result. The Dragon could feel inhibited by the Dog's more cautionary and measured approach. Rather than struggle on, these two will often prefer to go their own separate ways.

In love, again the prospects are not good. Although the Dragon may value the loyal and caring ways of the Dog, he will find it hard to cope with his sometimes anxious nature or to realize that the Dog needs someone who is prepared to listen to him and to understand. These two may try, but with such different personalities and interests, their relationship will be difficult.

~ With a Pig

The Dragon has a great fondness for the lively, genial and well-meaning Pig and relations between them will be good.

In the parent–child relationship, the Pig child will find much to admire and emulate in the Dragon parent and will strive to please. He will learn well and there will be a close and loving bond between parent and child.

As colleagues, their enthusiasm, determination and ideas will take them far. They like and trust each other, with the Dragon especially appreciating the Pig's commercial flair and sheer persistence. Both know they have it in them to achieve, and achieve they will. They are set on success and will not rest until they have achieved their aims.

In love, the Dragon and Pig understand each other well and have so much to share. Their interests and outlooks are similar and the Dragon will value having such a trusting, affectionate and generally joyful partner. They are ideally suited.

SUCCESS THROUGH LIFE

Bold, enterprising and forever active, the Dragon will have an often eventful life. Over the years he can look forward to some great successes, made all the more heartening as he will have had to strive hard to achieve them. There will also have been misjudgements, when the Dragon's sometimes rash and impulsive nature will have caused problems. However, the Dragon learns well and despite the occasional and almost inevitable setback, throughout his life he will be moving forward, always thirsting for new challenges and for ways in which he can use his skills and realize his potential. Life invariably gets better as he grows older.

As a child, the Dragon's adventurous and yet independent streak will soon show itself. Lively, strong-willed and often with a keen imagination, the young Dragon learns fast and well. While he will be respectful of those around him, he likes to forge his own way. Unlike some, the Dragon child is not one for mollycoddling and neither will he feel comfortable in too restrictive an environment. He needs a certain amount of space and freedom to experiment by himself. The Dragon's childhood can be filled with wonder and excitement, but also frustration, particularly when he feels prevented from doing what he would like.

Similarly, as he enters into adulthood, the Dragon could find it sometimes difficult to realize his hopes and ambitions. So full of ideas and keen to prove himself, he can experience some hard knocks. His ideals do not always fit in with harsh reality and it is at this time that he may have to face up to some bitter truths as he learns to adapt to the world as it is rather than as he would like it to be. However, while his late teens and early twenties can be a difficult time, the Dragon has a strong spirit and, sometimes after several false starts, will eventually find his way and start to carve out his niche.

In his working life, the Dragon's middle and older years are likely to be the more successful, especially as by then he will have tempered his more impulsive nature and be more experienced at promoting both himself and his ideas.

The Dragon's personal life will also be challenging in his early adult years. If he marries young, he will take his responsibilities seriously and will work hard to provide for his loved ones. While many Dragons can find happiness sharing life with a partner, they may not always find it that easy to adjust to their new role.

It is for this reason, as well as to preserve a certain degree of independence, that some Dragons prefer to remain single.

The Dragon's middle and older years will certainly see him wiser and a little mellower; it is from their forties onwards that most Dragons will find greater fulfilment. Also, by this time the Dragon will have learnt from any mistakes he may have made, particularly in being too rash or hasty.

In his more advanced years, the Dragon will often still be active, maintaining wide interests and enjoying the fruits of his labours. Although he may never be one for a great deal of reflection, should he come to look back over his years, he will often be surprised – and delighted – by all he has achieved and the various twists and turns his life has taken. So much will have been due to his efforts, style and the unshakable belief that he has in himself and his destiny.

FAMOUS DRAGONS

Louisa May Alcott, Maya Angelou, Lord Archer, Joan Baez, Count Basie, Pat Benatar, Maeve Binchy, Sandra Bullock, Julie Christie, James Coburn, Courteney Cox, Bing Crosby, Russell Crowe, Roald Dahl, Salvador Dali, Charles Darwin, Neil Diamond, Bo Diddley, Matt Dillon, Christian Dior, Placido Domingo, Fats Domino, Kirk Douglas, Faye Dunaway, Anatole France, Sigmund Freud, Graham Greene, Che Guevara, David Hasselhoff, Paul Hogan, Joan of Arc, Tom Jones, Helen Keller, Martin Luther King, Eartha Kitt, John Lennon, Abraham Lincoln, Queen Margrethe II of Denmark, Hosni Mubarak, Frederich Nietzsche, Florence Nightingale, Nick Nolte, Al Pacino, Gregory Peck, Pele, Edgar Allan Poe, Vladimir Putin, Christopher Reeve, Keanu Reeves, Sir Cliff Richard, Harold Robbins, George Bernard Shaw, Ringo Starr, Karlheinz

Stockhausen, Shirley Temple, Maria von Trapp, Andy Warhol, Johnny Weissmuller, Raquel Welch, the Earl of Wessex, Mae West.

SUCCESS TIPS FOR THE DRAGON

The Dragon is enterprising, gifted and imaginative. He is capable of coming up with many wonderful ideas. George Bernard Shaw, himself a Dragon, helped sum up the Dragon's pioneering approach when he wrote, 'You see things and say, "Why?" But I dream things that never were and I say, "Why not?" ' The Dragon should use his ability to think creatively and should promote his ideas. His input can make a considerable difference and can lead him to success.

The Dragon does possess an independent streak to his nature, however, and taken too far, this can prevent him from achieving all he might. In his dealings with others, he should try to listen to their views and feelings and be mindful of any advice he is given. Being too single-minded can deny him the backing he needs to advance. In certain situations, the Dragon should also choose his words more carefully. He does have a short temper and can be blunt and forthright, and again this can tell against him. The Dragon does need to handle his relations with others with consideration. He may be his own man, but success does depend upon the support of others and it is important not to jeopardize it.

The Dragon is very much caught up in the present, but it could also be in his interests to think about providing for his future. In particular, when he has funds he does not need, rather than succumb to the temptation to spend, he should save instead. An amount set aside on a regular basis can grow into a useful sum and the Dragon should give more thought to building up his assets for the longer term.

The Dragon lives life at a fast pace. He works hard and he plays hard. For him, life is very much to be lived. However, by being continually involved in whatever he is doing – and so often being intense about it – the Dragon can use up a great deal of energy and nervous tension and, as a result, can sometimes become prone to stress-related complaints. It would be in his interests to give himself the chance to regularly rest and unwind rather than drive himself so continually. He should give himself time to recharge his batteries, to relax, to think, to meditate and to be at one with the world. If he can regularly inject some tranquillity into his often busy life, he will feel (and often do) so much better as a result.

Similarly, the Dragon likes to be active but sometimes he can spread his energies too widely. This can lead to mistakes and to more pressure as well as prevent proper attention being given to his most essential tasks. There will be occasions when the Dragon will need to be more self-disciplined, limit his commitments and concentrate on his priorities. Focused attention on what needs to be done can lead to far better results than attempting too much. To be more successful, the Dragon should stick to his objectives and to what he does best. That way he is also likely to achieve the high standards he continually seeks.

SOME FINAL THOUGHTS FROM DRAGONS

To accomplish great things, we must not only act, but also dream, not only plan, but also believe.
Anatole France

We can do anything we want to do if we stick to it long enough.
Helen Keller

Life is either a daring adventure or nothing.
Helen Keller

Determine that the thing can and shall be done, and then we shall find the way.
Abraham Lincoln

Always bear in mind that your own resolution to success is more than any other one thing.
Abraham Lincoln

Either you reach a higher point today, or you exercise your strength in order to be able to climb higher tomorrow.
Frederich Nietzsche

He who has a WHY to live can bear with almost any HOW.
Frederich Nietzsche

Far away there in the sunshine are my highest aspirations. I may not reach them, but I can look up and see their beauty, believe in them and try to follow where they lead.
Louisa May Alcott

Everything happens to everybody sooner or later if there is time enough.
George Bernard Shaw

Life is not a 'brief candle'. It is a splendid torch that I want to make burn as brightly as possible before handing on to future generations.
George Bernard Shaw

The
Snake

Although the Snake may lie curled up, silent and motionless, its presence is still very evident. Perhaps this is due to its reputation, its sleek and distinctive appearance or the knowledge that at any moment it could suddenly spring into action. The Snake has aura, mystery and the ability to mesmerize. And so it is with those born under the sixth Chinese sign.

Snakes are quiet, reflective and deep thinkers. They like to keep their own counsel and while they may not be as outgoing as some, they are strong-willed and ambitious. The Snake is also blessed with a very patient nature and is often prepared to bide his time waiting for the right moment to strike. When that moment arrives, he will act with such focus, will-power and ingenuity that he often secures his aims.

The Snake is wise, astute and highly intuitive. Some Snakes are even psychic, with a strong sense of how certain actions will work out and what is the right course for them. Throughout his life, the Snake remains very much his own master and relies on his own intuition.

In his manner the Snake tends to be quietly spoken and can appear reserved. He is certainly no chatterbox and dislikes small talk and idle gossip, preferring his conversations to have meaning and relevance. He can be profound in his thoughts and yet often laces what he says with his own distinctive brand of humour. It is because he is such a deep thinker and yet has a lighter touch that others find him so engaging. At times he can be mesmerizing.

The Snake is not one for wasting energy. Some signs can get distracted and meddle in all sorts of activities, not so the Snake. He has clear objectives and remains dedicated and focused. He also tends only to act after much careful thought. He is well organized and methodical.

However, while the Snake is capable of achieving great success, he does have several flaws which not only work against him but can also cause him much personal anguish. In particular, while he may appear outwardly calm, inwardly he can be highly strung and full of nervous energy which he is forever bottling up. Because he keeps his innermost feelings to himself, they can sometimes have a debilitating effect, sapping his mental energy and making him feel stressed, frustrated or worried. For this reason, the Snake really would find it helpful to be more open about his feelings. As he will find, problems shared can so often be halved.

Another failing, again stemming from his reserved nature, is that the Snake does not like taking advice from others. He prefers to stick to his own ideas and so closes his mind to what could be useful input from others. Again, he does need to be more receptive to others' willingness to help him.

Due to the care the Snake takes with his various activities, he does not take setbacks or rejection well. If his plans do not work out, the effects can, for a time, unsettle his confidence and he is a bad loser. Should anyone do him wrong, he will not forgive and at times can be capable of considerable vindictiveness. An angered Snake can indeed be venomous!

However, while the Snake does have his negative traits, by being prepared to lose some of his reserve (and this is something he does need to work at), he can find his life and level of success improving a great deal.

Another notable feature of the Snake's character is that he is prepared to be different. He is capable of much original thought and there have been quite a few Snakes who have achieved success by furthering their own distinctive talents and ideas. The Snake is a creator and this, combined with his dedicated approach, will often enable him to go far in life. And the Snake does desire success, not least for the benefits it can bring. He likes the finer things in life, aims for quality and is never one to deprive himself of anything he may want. The Snake can be indulgent and at times acquisitive. Living in style is, he feels, just reward for his efforts.

Both the male and female Snake possess excellent taste. They have an eye for detail and for quality. In appearance, both can be smart and stylish, with the female often adorning herself and her clothes with items of jewellery. She knows what suits her. In addition, she carries herself in a calm, serene and confident way which others find attractive. She has a keen and alert mind and is supremely efficient, both in her work and the organization of her home.

The male Snake too is a keen organizer and likes to plan his activities with the utmost care. Although he keeps his ideas very much to himself, he is often very clear in his own mind about what he wants to achieve in life. The male Snake is a great one for planning and contemplating his destiny. He is quiet, well mannered and careful in both what he says and does. He is certainly not one to be hurried against his will or to make decisions on the spur of the moment. He is a deliberator and he moves at his own pace. And, despite his reserved and thoughtful nature, he often possesses a rich humour.

Both the male and female choose their friends carefully. Rather than having a large social circle, the Snake prefers to have a few close and loyal friends. He likes to build up trust and rapport and can become particularly possessive over his loved ones. Should they ever let him down or give him cause for jealousy, he can feel this deeply. The Snake demands loyalty and exclusivity. However, he can himself be guilty of double standards, with the male in particular having a roving eye, especially in his early adult years. It is for this reason that the Snake should not settle down at too early an age but instead enjoy his freedom and the passions of youth. The Snake does have a strong sexual drive.

When he does settle down, he will greatly enjoy setting up his home and stamping it with his personality. There will be plenty of books, for he tends to be an avid reader, and he will also enjoy adding more aesthetic touches, including attractive pictures, objects or antiques. He will sometimes opt for what can be distinctive décor and his taste for the unusual and for quality will be evident.

The Snake greatly enjoys family life and makes an especially good parent. With his rich imagination and humour, he relates well to children and will enjoy the time he spends with them, both joining in with their games and encouraging their various activities. Admittedly, he will not care for the traumas that sometimes go with family life and may not be the most effective disciplinarian – stern words do not fit in with his generally placid and easy-going manner – but the Snake will strive to make his family a close and loving unit.

In addition to his family and work, the Snake will always be keen to maintain his own personal interests. As well as books, he generally enjoys the arts and whether music, the theatre, cinema or art itself, the Snake appreciates creativity. He can also be drawn to deep and more questioning subjects, including the unknown, the paranormal and mysteries of the universe. The Snake is a great ponderer! He could also be a keen photographer, particularly of places of beauty that he visits, as well as enjoy opportunities just to reflect, perhaps while out walking or in some other quiet (and often solitary) pursuit.

It is considered that Snakes born in summer, especially when conditions are hot, fare better than those born in winter. But wise, determined and so much his own master, the Snake will, throughout his often long life, forge his own path and do so with style and originality.

SUCCESS AND WORK

The Snake is a deliberator. He plans, he organizes and he invariably knows where he is heading. He is both shrewd and astute and by using his skills to good effect, he can do well.

The Snake has a good business head and he relies a lot on intuition, careful preparation and persistence. Some may be tempted to give up at the first sign of difficulty, not so the Snake. He is patient and determined. He knows what he wants and is prepared to acquire the skills necessary to achieve his aims. If this takes many years, the Snake will accept it. He has vision – and sometimes thinks very much in the long term. He succeeds because he acts with such purpose.

In choosing a career, the Snake should avoid those that involve being in a frenzied or pressurized atmosphere. He likes to plan ahead and is not suited to making sudden decisions. Nor is he suited to excessively physical types of work. His energy levels do not tend to be that high and after bouts of intense work or activity, he does need time to regain his strength and thoughts. The Snake is better suited to more cerebral activities, often those that require training and specialist skills. He particularly enjoys research and, having an analytical mind, can be attracted to science, technology, medicine and the financial sector. Being such a deep and profound thinker, the Snake could also be drawn to the Church or astrology, psychology or counselling work.

The Snake can also make a name for himself promoting his own distinctive style, particularly in art, music and literature. His original approach and enquiring mind can set him apart from others and bring him success in his chosen field. His eye for quality and his fine taste can also serve him well should he wish to become a retailer, particularly of more exclusive products.

The Snake is certainly capable of making an impression in his chosen line of work and doing well. However, as with other aspects of his life, he does need to overcome his somewhat reserved nature and be more outgoing. He certainly has the talents and capabilities, but to succeed he cannot ignore personnel skills either. In order to progress, the Snake does need to pay more attention to his relations with his colleagues and build up contacts rather than being too much of a lone figure.

However, in his work, the Snake *is* very much his own master. Once he has decided on the path to follow, he will pursue this with dedication, resolve and persistence. Despite his quiet and placid demeanour, he is always alert, keenly ambitious and, when the time is ready, will advance. The Snake has it within him to be a great success.

SUCCESS AND MONEY

The Snake likes money. It enables him to live in style. And he is usually successful in money matters, with many Snakes being financially secure in their later years.

As with so much in life, the Snake likes to plan ahead and many Snakes will save regularly and so build up their assets. Also, with his abilities to analyse situations and sense opportunities, the Snake can be a shrewd investor, particularly in identifying good investment opportunities. However, he should be wary of gambling. Maybe it is the pressure of having to make a snap decision on not always reliable evidence, but his wily instinct seems to desert him then and he has the reputation for being the worst gambler in the Chinese zodiac.

Gambling apart, the Snake is usually fortunate in money matters and with sound investments, good planning and hard work, he is certainly capable of building up great wealth. He does, though, possess an indulgent streak and enjoys spending on himself. He regards personal treats just recompense for his hard work. He is also most generous towards his loved ones and will delight in buying them presents and ensuring they have all they need. However, it is with his nearest and dearest that his spending tends to stop. Outside his inner circle, the Snake can be careful with his money and to some may even appear miserly. But he very much likes to be in control of his assets and to use them in the way he thinks fit.

The Snake can sometimes improve his financial situation by furthering his ideas. It has been said that it takes just one idea to make a fortune and the Snake certainly has it within him to profit from his often original concepts. Indeed, some of the world's richest people have been Snakes. The Snake certainly possesses the skills and attributes necessary to become financially secure.

SUCCESS AND LOVE

Quiet, thoughtful and so alluring, the Snake has an almost irresistible nature. So many can fall under his spell, charmed by his softly spoken manner, his style, gentle humour and intelligence. The Snake draws people in and does not let go of them easily. He is possessive, expecting loyalty and devotion. Should his partner ever give him grounds for jealousy, he will feel it deeply, so much so that in some cases the relationship could be seriously undermined.

The Snake is exclusive and because he expects his partner to enter and exist within his own world, he will choose that person with great care. Ideally, he will seek someone not only to love but also to be a confidante and friend. He will want someone he can have meaningful discussions with, someone who has similar tastes and who enjoys a settled and refined lifestyle. For the Snake, there must be a meeting of minds and an intellectual as well as physical compatibility. He does not make decisions lightly and he will choose his partner only after lengthy and careful thought. He is never one for rushing into commitments.

The one word of warning that must be sounded is that some Snakes can be guilty of double standards and while expecting so much of others, they can nevertheless yield to temptation all too readily. When in a relationship, to act in any way that could undermine it could jeopardize so much. Snakes so tempted, do heed these words well.

In some ways the Snake can be so solitary and yet he cannot exist without others and passion is important to him. When in love with someone he can share his thoughts and hopes with, he will find his life so much richer as a result.

SUCCESS WITH OTHERS

The Snake may be quiet and reserved, but he certainly knows how to intrigue. Those he meets are often fascinated by his complex personality – one moment he can be witty and frivolous, the next profound and intense. And the Snake does not yield his secrets easily. It takes others time to get to know him well and he does choose his friends and associates with care. In his relationships with others he is looking for trust, loyalty and a meeting of minds. He will find there are some signs that he relates to far better than others.

With a Rat

The Snake thinks a great deal of the clever and resourceful Rat and relations between them will be good.

In the parent–child relationship, the Snake parent will enjoy the lively and imaginative ways of the Rat child, with the young Rat responding well to Snake parent's calm, collected and caring manner. There will be a close and loving bond between them.

As colleagues, the Snake and Rat work well together, with the Snake appreciating and benefiting from the Rat's drive, enthusiasm and enterprise. The Snake sometimes needs an active business associate to help him realize his potential and the Rat can, in that respect, prove ideal. Each brings out the best in the other, with their ideas, resourcefulness and ambition often leading them to considerable success.

In love, the Snake and Rat mean much to each other. Both seek a settled and secure home life and they will enjoy a particularly close relationship with many interests in common. These two are good for each other, with the Snake often becoming more sociable as a result of the Rat's influence. He will also appreciate the Rat's warm and attentive manner. They can make a happy match.

⟋⟍ With an Ox

The Snake has a great respect for the quiet, resolute and determined Ox and relations between the two signs will be good.

In the parent–child relationship, the Snake parent will admire the quiet and conscientious ways of the Ox child. There will be a close bond between them, with the Ox child doing much to please his thoughtful and caring Snake parent.

As colleagues, the Snake and Ox trust and respect each other and will work well together. Both are determined to make much of their skills and their patience, persistence and will-power will so often bring them the success they seek. The Snake will gain strength from the Ox's tenacious and resolute nature and together they make a powerful combination.

In love, the Snake and Ox feel at ease with each other. Both have generally quiet and placid natures as well as a fond appreciation of the finer things in life. The Snake will especially value the Ox's dependable, sincere and caring ways. Sharing many interests as well as pouring much energy into their home life, they are well suited and can make a successful match.

⟋⟍ With a Tiger

Being of a quiet and placid nature, the Snake will find the active and energetic lifestyle of the Tiger does not sit comfortably with him and relations between these two signs are poor.

In the parent–child relationship, the Snake parent could find the young Tiger's exuberant and self-willed ways difficult, and while the pair may try to get along, relations between them will be tricky and need much care on both sides.

As colleagues, these two will again clash. The Tiger is a dynamo, always geared up for action, while the Snake prefers to work according to a plan and proceed at a much more measured pace. With such different approaches, these two will quickly become exasperated with each other and prefer to go their separate ways.

In love, the Snake may initially be attracted by the Tiger's warm, lively and generous personality, but the Tiger likes to live life to the full and to keep active, while the Snake is more for a quiet and settled existence. Being so possessive, he will also find it hard to cope with the Tiger's more independent ways. If this relationship is to work, a great many allowances will need to be made. Tradition does not augur well.

With a Rabbit

With often similar interests and attitudes, the Snake gets on well with the Rabbit and relations between these two signs are good.

In the parent–child relationship, the calm and loving ways of the Snake parent are much appreciated by the young Rabbit, who will strive to please. There will be a good bond between them.

As colleagues, both are shrewd and have good business sense. However, both are also cautious and they will sometimes lack the energy and assertiveness that some enterprises require. As planners and deliberators they will be fine, but when it comes to action, problems could occur. The potential for success is there but so much hinges upon the conditions and the type of business they are in.

In love, there is considerable attraction between the Snake and Rabbit and they can find much happiness together. Both seek a calm, settled and orderly lifestyle as well as savour the finer things in life. With many interests in common these two are often on the same wavelength and there will be a good rapport between them. They are ideally suited.

⚮ With a Dragon

There is a good chemistry between the Snake and Dragon and relations between these two signs are often excellent.

In the parent–child relationship, the Snake parent will delight in encouraging and sharing so much with a keen and receptive Dragon child. There will be great love between them.

As colleagues, they will respect each other's individual talents and together can achieve great success. The Snake will feel inspired by the Dragon's often infectious enthusiasm as well as appreciate having such a confident and redoubtable associate. They make a strong and worthy team.

In love, such bliss and happiness. These two signs really are attracted to each other, both on a mental and physical level. It is as if they are made for each other, with each finding the other such fascinating and enjoyable company. They will love and support each other and both will benefit. In particular, the Snake is likely to become more outgoing and outwardly confident with the Dragon's support as well as more action-oriented. Provided the Dragon never gives the Snake grounds for jealousy, theirs will be an excellent and enduring match.

⚮ With another Snake

A meeting of two great thinkers. With their often similar outlooks and interests, two Snakes can, for a time, get on well.

In the parent–child relationship, the Snake parent is well placed to understand a Snake child. However, even he could find it difficult to penetrate the young Snake's quiet and reserved nature. The young Snake does, after all, need time to blossom and gain confidence. Relations will improve as the Snake child develops and the bond between parent and child will become stronger.

As colleagues, two Snakes may have ideas and good business skills, but the Snake is by nature cautious and given to much deliberation, so he really needs to work with someone who is more dynamic and geared up for action. Two Snakes together could be too ponderous and as a result may not be the most effective or successful of teams.

In love, two Snakes will fascinate each other. There will be passion and intensity and, with their fine tastes, they will aim to live in great style. However, while they can be so much in love, they are possessive and their jealous natures could easily be aroused. Should any suspicions enter into their relationship, cracks would soon start to appear. It has been said that two Snakes do have difficulty living under the same roof and the longer term prospects for this match could indeed be tricky.

With a Horse

Although the Snake thinks well of the Horse, they live their lives in different ways and relations between the two signs will be reasonable rather than close.

In the parent–child relationship, relations between Snake parent and Horse child will need to be handled with care. The Snake parent, usually calm and relatively easy-going, could find the Horse child's independent and strong-willed ways a challenge. To build up a satisfactory rapport will need time and a certain goodwill on both sides.

As colleagues, the Snake and Horse can learn from each other. In particular, the Snake will benefit from the Horse's more action-oriented approach. By combining their considerable skills and ideas, they can often make an effective team.

In love, the initial attraction could be strong. There will be passion and great excitement as each explores the other's world. They are both deep thinkers and enjoy intelligent discussion. The Snake will also appreciate the Horse's loyal and affectionate nature. However, the Horse is strong-willed, has a volatile nature and prefers a more active lifestyle to that of the placid Snake. For this relationship to endure, both signs will need to adapt. This can prove a challenging match.

With a Goat

With their easy-going natures and mutual interests, the Snake and Goat get on well together.

In the parent–child relationship, the Goat child will respond well to the Snake parent's calm yet attentive guidance. With their similar interests, too, there will be a good understanding between them.

As colleagues, these two have synergy! Both are creative and imaginative and each will support the other. The Snake will particularly value the Goat's creative input and when they put their ideas into practice, their often innovative approach can make quite an impact.

In love, the Snake and Goat enjoy a wonderful rapport. Both seek a secure, stable and peaceful existence and with so many interests to share and an appreciation of the good life, they can make a blissful match. The Snake will especially value the kindly and considerate nature of the Goat as well as his often gentle humour. They are well suited.

With a Monkey

The Snake finds the Monkey fascinating company and in most cases relations between these two signs can go well.

In the parent–child relationship, the Snake parent will delight in the young Monkey's enterprising and joyful nature (both signs have a good sense of humour) and will guide him well. There will be a good rapport between them.

As colleagues, relations will be more difficult. The Snake, so methodical and cautious, will be wary of the Monkey's often hasty and, to his mind, sometimes reckless approach. The Monkey likes action, relies a lot on his wits and can be crafty, and this does not sit comfortably with the Snake. In work matters there will be mistrust and a general lack of accord between them.

In love, however, the Snake and Monkey are well matched. As both are so curious and yet tend to be secretive, each will delight in discovering the other's rich and deep personality and in the process they will build up a close bond. They understand and complement each other well, with the Snake enjoying the Monkey's *joie de vivre*, loyalty and charm, as well as sharing many of his interests.

With a Rooster

The Snake has a great liking for the well-organized and wise Rooster and the two signs get on well together.

In the parent–child relationship, the Snake parent will admire the Rooster child's keen and methodical nature and the young Rooster will respond well to the Snake's calm, thoughtful and attentive manner. There will be a good understanding between them.

As colleagues, the Snake and Rooster make an effective combination. Both are keen planners as well as orderly and methodical. However, they also have their individual strengths and by combining these, they can enjoy a good level of success. The Snake will particularly benefit from the Rooster's more assertive nature and his help in setting some of his ideas in motion. The Rooster is a good prodder for the Snake!

In love, the Snake and Rooster make an excellent match. These two have style, elegance and often similar outlooks and interests. They understand each other and will value each other's support. The Snake will especially appreciate the Rooster's sincerity and trust and will be pleased to have such an efficient, conscientious and orderly partner. They are well suited.

With a Dog

Once these signs have overcome their initial reserve and got to know each other better, they can build up a good rapport.

In the parent–child relationship the Snake parent will be a good influence on the young Dog. Understanding the Dog child's anxious nature, the Snake parent will, through his calm, caring and supportive manner, do much to build up his confidence. There will be a great bond between them.

As colleagues, though, the Snake and Dog do not make a good combination. Both are cautious in their undertakings and to thrive the Snake really needs a colleague who is prepared to take action rather than simply worry. They may like each other, but in a working relationship getting results will not be easy.

In love, the prospects are significantly better. The Snake will value the Dog's faithful and caring ways and be able to trust him – and to the Snake this is just so important. Admittedly there will be differences they will need to reconcile and the Snake will need to be tolerant of the Dog's sometimes anxious nature, but with care they can make a loving match.

～ With a Pig

The Pig is expansive, the Snake secretive, and herein lies the problem with this relationship. These two signs do not relate well to each other.

In the parent–child relationship, the Snake parent will, though, appreciate the young Pig's willing and genial nature and do much to encourage him as well as enjoy sharing many interests. It is at this level that relations between the two signs will be at their best.

As colleagues, there could be a distinct lack of accord. The Pig will be wary of the Snake's guarded manner and tendency to keep his thoughts to himself, while the Snake will sometimes feel the Pig is too impulsive. Without trust and a satisfactory rapport, the Snake and Pig do not make a good team.

In love, relations can be challenging. The Pig is open and outgoing, the Snake secretive and reserved. Although both appreciate the finer things in life and can learn much from each other, their natures are so very different that there will need to be considerable goodwill and some major adjustments if their relationship is to endure. The portents are not good.

SUCCESS THROUGH LIFE

The Snake takes life at a measured pace. He progresses slowly but surely, tenaciously working towards his aims. It is because he is so patient and persistent that his life will often be crowned with considerable achievement.

As a child the Snake is usually very self-contained, amusing himself with imaginative games and devoting hours to his often specific interests. He can be a solitary child, a loner, but if his home life is settled and he has the love and support of those around him, his formative years can be happy ones.

In his early teens years the Snake could, though, experience a few tricky and disappointing years. Often a late developer, he could find himself struggling in certain subjects at school or feel (partly as a result of his solitary nature) that he is not involved in the social scene as much as he would like. However, by his mid to late teens, this will change, particularly as by then he will be much more inspired by certain parts of his education and will have formed some closer friendships.

When he leaves his parental home, the Snake's life could again go through another tricky period. Young Snakes often lack confidence and do not assert themselves enough. Also, at this stage some Snakes may not be quite sure of the career they wish to follow and could go through a succession of jobs before they find their forte. Once found, the Snake's quest will begin, with years of training, specialization and effort ahead. Just as the Snake himself tends to be a late developer, sometimes his career does not really start to take off until his thirties and beyond. Success for the Snake so often comes after years of application and here his patience and persistence are so valuable.

In his late teenage years the Snake will also be grappling with the complexities of love. Popular with the opposite sex, he will enjoy himself, but his jealous and possessive nature will often bring him pain. It would indeed be wise for the Snake not to settle down at too young an age but wait until he is more established as well as more emotionally mature.

As the years pass, life will often improve for the Snake. If he becomes a parent, he will revel in the upbringing of his children as well as strive to make his home life settled and content. Middle and old age can be a satisfying and often successful time for the Snake as by now he will have found his calling in life and grown in confidence, and by becoming more assertive he will have been able to make more of himself and his ideas. The Snake's good financial sense will also enable many Snakes to be materially well off and able to enjoy a good standard of living in their later years.

Thoughtful, self-willed and strongly motivated, the Snake will not find life's journey always easy, especially as he will choose to forge his own route. But, despite the loneliness of some of his endeavours and the knocks he will sometimes face, his life is often one of great achievement – and crafted very much in his own individual style.

FAMOUS SNAKES

Muhammad Ali, Ann-Margret, Yasser Arafat, Lord Baden-Powell, Kim Basinger, Bjork, Tony Blair, Heinrich Böll, Brahms, Pierce Brosnan, Casanova, Chubby Checker, Dick Cheney, Fyodor Dostoevsky, Bob Dylan, Sir Edward Elgar, Sir Alexander Fleming, Henry Fonda, Mahatma Gandhi, Greta Garbo, Art Garfunkel, J. Paul Getty, Dizzy Gillespie, Goethe, Princess Grace of Monaco, Stephen Hawking, Audrey Hepburn, Jack Higgins, Howard Hughes, Tom Hulce, Liz Hurley, James Joyce, Stacy Keach, Ronan Keating, J. F. Kennedy, Carole King, Cyndi Lauper, Lennox Lewis, Mao Tse-tung, Henri Matisse, Robert Mitchum, Nasser, Alfred Nobel, Ryan O'Neal, Mike Oldfield, Aristotle Onassis, Jacqueline Onassis, Pablo Picasso, Mary Pickford, Brad Pitt, Franklin D. Roosevelt, Mickey Rourke, Jean-Paul Sartre, Franz Schubert, Brooke Shields, Paul Simon, John Thaw, Madame Tussaud, Dionne Warwick, Charlie Watts, Oprah Winfrey, P. G. Wodehouse, Virginia Woolf, Susannah York.

SUCCESS TIPS FOR THE SNAKE

The Snake is a great planner, but sometimes he can be just too cautious in his undertakings and could miss out on opportunities or lose momentum. The Snake should be careful that he does not lose out because he deliberates too long. In some instances he needs to seize the moment. It is, after all, those who take action who get results.

In his younger years the Snake could find himself lacking confidence in certain situations. Confidence tends to come with experience and until the Snake has that experience he should trust himself and hold faith with his abilities. Even if he feels shy, nervous or ill at ease in some situations, he should draw on his inner reserves and be bold. As Goethe, himself a Snake, wrote, boldness has genius, magic and power in it, and by being bold the Snake will discover these qualities and more.

Because he tends to be quiet and reserved, the Snake can sometimes lose out to those who may be more outgoing and assertive. While the Snake may not wish to change his nature, he can certainly improve his prospects by paying closer attention to his relations with others, especially his colleagues and business associates. Although he may be a loner, he needs to build up contacts and pay attention to the views and feelings of others. In order to progress, it *is* necessary to have the support and approval of others and, to be successful, the Snake must be prepared to seek this.

The Snake is very much one for keeping his feelings to himself, but sometimes his tendency to dwell on certain aspects of his life can cause him great anguish. In particular, if he has been wronged or feels jealous, he can let this gnaw away at him and affect his very being. And he makes the situation worse by thinking so much about it. Whenever the Snake finds himself dwelling on the negative, he should make every effort to direct his thoughts towards more constructive areas of his life. He is, after all, the master of his own thoughts. Also, he would be helped by being more forthcoming and talking over his anxieties and feelings with others. Sometimes he will find his worries (and imaginings) can be eased in the very process of discussion.

Also, the Snake possesses a deep and inquiring mind and as a result he is capable of coming up with some profound ideas. Rather than keep them to himself, he should release them and see what happens. They could bring far greater results than he ever imagined. The Snake is an original thinker and throughout his life, he should make much of his ideas.

SOME FINAL THOUGHTS FROM SNAKES

Happiness lies in the joy of achievement and the thrill of creative effort.
Franklin D. Roosevelt

The only limit to our realization of tomorrow will be our doubts of today. Let us move forward with strong and active faith.
Franklin D. Roosevelt

To reach a port, we must sail – sail, not tie at anchor, sail, not drift.
Franklin D. Roosevelt

If you want to be respected, the great thing is to respect yourself.
Fyodor Dostoevsky

A man is a success if he gets up in the morning and gets to bed
at night, and in between he does what he wants to do.
Bob Dylan

Just trust yourself, then you will know how to live.
Johann Wolfgang von Goethe

Whatever you can do or dream, you can begin it.
Boldness has genius, magic and power in it.
Begin it now.
Johann Wolfgang von Goethe

The
Horse

Whether being ridden for pleasure or for sport, pulling carriages or carts, the Horse has proved a valuable companion to man. Easy to get on with and hard-working, the Horse possesses many likeable qualities and these are so often found in those born under the seventh Chinese sign.

Horses are governed by the signs of elegance and ardour and both traits are very evident. The Horse takes great pride in his appearance and carries himself well and with style. As far as looks are concerned he certainly knows how to impress and often makes a striking figure. Also, the Horse possesses a lively spirit. Always active, always eager to be involved, he has a practical nature as well as a quick and sharp mind. He enjoys being the centre of attention and in most situations will make his presence felt.

The Horse is a skilful communicator and with his often wide range of interests, is able to talk well on many topics. He can be a persuasive and sometimes amusing speaker and his often lively repartee helps others to warm to him. He enjoys company and has a friendly and outgoing nature.

The Horse certainly possesses many qualities which will serve him well. However he also has his faults and these can, if not watched, undermine his level of success. In particular, the Horse can be hasty and impatient. He lives for the moment and likes to get results fast. Should obstacles arise or he feels he is not making the headway he would like, he will often give up and turn his attention to something else. The Horse lacks staying power and sometimes he will abandon his current activities (regardless of all the time and effort he may have already put in) for something which will bring more immediate results. There will certainly be times in the Horse's life when perseverance would have brought better results. This tendency to give up too easily can also lead the Horse to change his jobs quite frequently and, certainly in his early adult life, he could lose out because he has not given himself the chance to establish himself and find his own niche.

The Horse's desire to be involved and be the centre of attention can also cause him problems. He can be hasty, impulsive and sometimes carried away in the heat of the moment, and whether through talking too much, giving away secrets (which the Horse finds hard to keep) or acting in a reckless manner, he will certainly come to regret his actions or words from time to time. He can also lose his temper easily, sometimes over comparatively petty matters, and while he may think his outbursts will quickly pass, they can linger in the minds of those who have to endure them and can harm the Horse's reputation.

As the Horse matures he will find he is better able to control some of his more negative traits, but throughout he does need to watch his impatience as well as his temper.

In all his activities the Horse needs to feel that he has the support and approval of others. He is not one for a solitary existence or for feeling isolated. When he does have support and feels inspired, he can truly excel. In his work, the Horse can be willing to put in long hours in order to meet deadlines or his objectives and if he allows himself the time to nurture his own special talents, he will certainly enjoy success in both his life and work.

With his outgoing nature, the Horse relates well to others. He has charm, good humour and often good looks. Because he makes such popular and interesting company, he will rarely lack friends or admirers. And the Horse can give all for love. When smitten, he is capable of doing anything to win and keep the heart of his loved one. He loves being in love and being loved. However, while a relationship may absorb and almost consume him, when those initial fiery passions begin to wane, he will sometimes move to new pastures. He does, certainly in his early years, possess a flirtatious streak and is likely to have a string of (often serious) romances.

The Horse tends to marry young – sometimes too young. Here again his hastiness can sometimes be to his detriment. While some marriages made early will endure and bring great happiness, there are nevertheless those Horses who will regret their decision and marry again or settle down with another partner.

Although the Horse will make sure his home is comfortable and well equipped, he is not one for spending a great deal of time there. He does not like housework – he is not the tidiest or most organized of people – and much prefers going out socializing, devoting time to his interests and generally keeping himself active. Sitting for hours by the fireside is just not his style, unless, that is, he is able to hold forth on some topic surrounded by family and friends.

The male Horse certainly knows how to impress. Often smart in appearance, he has charm and presence and makes an interesting speaker. However, he does have a restless side to his nature and sometimes spreads his energies too widely. He also tries hard to win the approval of others and can at times be vain and self-centred. But he is generally good-humoured, loyal to family and friends and generous with both his time and money.

The female Horse also makes much of herself. With often excellent dress sense and an interest in fashion as well as an eye for quality, she has style and grace. She also keeps herself active with a wide range of interests as well as maintaining an often large group of friends. A keen socializer, she makes a great conversationalist, possesses a ready wit and has a good understanding of human nature. However, she does have a carefree manner and does not particularly like a narrow or mundane lifestyle. Neither does she tend to be the most punctual of people! She is, though, well liked and uses her considerable abilities to good effect, particularly in her chosen career.

If the Horse becomes a parent, he will enjoy encouraging his children with their interests and will be particularly effective in bringing out their individual talents. He will also try to imbue them with a sense of adventure and independence, realizing that one day they must seek their own destiny. The Horse will love his children, but is not one for fussing unnecessarily over them and should they annoy him then they will not be spared his temper.

As far as his interests are concerned, the Horse is a keen traveller. He enjoys exploring areas new to him as well as meeting those who live there. Travel appeals to his restless nature. He likes to roam free and to be able to go wherever the mood takes him. Whether as a backpacker, hiker or camper, the Horse enjoys freedom and the great outdoors.

He can also be a great sports enthusiast. Whether as a participant (and often, being agile and nimble, he can excel at sport) or as an onlooker, he will enjoy the excitement, adrenalin and vigour that sport can offer. He may also be fond of dancing and whether he chooses to dance in a sedate and graceful fashion or with energy and flamboyance, he can make a dashing figure on the dance floor. He usually has a good ear for music and many Horses obtain pleasure from playing an instrument. With his sociable nature, the Horse will also enjoy interests which he can share with others – he is not one for solitary pursuits – and if his interests allow him to be involved in a club or society, then he will play an important part. He always likes to be involved.

As the Horse has such a lively temperament and keeps himself so active, his life will invariably be rich and varied. There are aspects of his character which can tell against him, notably his impatience, volatility and quick temper, but once he can master these, then he can do well and achieve a great deal. Horses born in winter are generally considered the luckiest of their sign, but all Horses possess the personality, vigour and zest to lead an interesting and rewarding life.

SUCCESS AND WORK

The Horse is versatile, hard-working and keen and, when sufficiently motivated, is prepared to put in many long and irregular hours in order to secure his aims. In addition, the Horse has an effective way with others. A good communicator, he can persuade, convince and inspire. His desire to play a leading role in all he does can also help him to progress. He certainly has the talents and capabilities to achieve a great deal, but he does have some failings. Once he can address these, then he will find his career becoming more fulfilling and correspondingly more successful.

One of the Horse's chief weaknesses is his lack of staying power. Sometimes he gets diverted all too easily. He can start projects and pour a great deal of energy into them, only to abandon them if he finds something more interesting to do. Should uncertainties or obstacles start to loom, then again he can all too readily decide to move on. Sometimes he does not give himself enough time to become established or to master the skills necessary to make the progress he otherwise might.

Also, while the Horse may possess a creative mind and is capable of generating many useful ideas, he does not always make the most of them. It could be his fear of failure and possible loss of face that holds him back or his uncertainty about the best way to proceed, but in either case he should have more faith in himself. By advancing his ideas and winning support for them (and here his personable and persuasive manner will help), he could find they will reward him well.

Work-wise, especially in his early adult years, the Horse must learn to be more persevering and not be tempted to make so many changes. Although he may be eager to obtain results, sometimes these do require time and experience, and the Horse must accept this. As the saying goes, 'Rome was not built in a day.' Neither can the Horse's success be secured so easily. It is something he *will* need to strive for. Also, while no one likes failing, being rebuffed or having to face many difficulties, it is at these times that experience can be gained and lessons learnt, and the Horse must recognize this. As the Chinese proverb states, 'The gem cannot be polished without friction, nor man perfected without trials.'

However, once the Horse is prepared to work steadily towards his aims and to build up his expertise, he will find himself able to make headway in his chosen career. In particular he will enjoy positions which will bring him into contact with others and allow him to use his skills as a communicator as well as contain an element of variety. The Horse can make an effective teacher, journalist or media presenter. His love of travel and aptitude for mastering foreign languages could attract him to positions in the travel industry, in transport or as a company representative or spokesperson. His outgoing manner will also

serve him well if he chooses to enter the entertainment or cater-
ing industry, especially as these will allow him a certain freedom
to experiment and to use his personality to good effect.

With his agile and often athletic build, the Horse can also be
attracted to the world of sport, where some will enjoy considerable success.

When it comes to work, the Horse certainly possesses the
talents to go far. Hard-working, able, imaginative and a good communicator, he has much in his favour. But to realize his potential,
he does need to conquer his restless and volatile nature and be
prepared to persist. The road to success can sometimes be a long
one and the Horse must be prepared to accept this.

SUCCESS WITH MONEY

The Horse enjoys money, but rather than seeking great wealth,
he will usually be grateful for what he has. He is not greedy or
particularly materialistic. Instead he regards money as a tool,
one which he will quite happily use to fulfil his needs.

The Horse usually manages his money well and will always
try to ensure that his obligations are covered. What is left over
will be spent on his friends and loved ones – when in company
the Horse can be most generous – and on his various interests.
For the Horse, money is to be used and enjoyed.

There will, though, be times during the Horse's life when he
does struggle financially, especially in his early adult years when
he not only takes on new commitments but could also change
his job quite frequently or face periods of unemployment. But
even though times may sometimes be hard, the Horse is
resourceful and can manage on limited means. He does not
need money or indeed material possessions to make him happy;
what he values more is the freedom to go his own way.

However, while the Horse is not particularly materialistic and does not tend to think too far ahead, he could find it will help him to set funds aside for his future. Even if this is just a small amount each month, over time it can become a valuable asset. Neither should the Horse neglect his insurance cover. Failure to be properly insured, whether for medical purposes, travel or the home, could sometimes leave the Horse financially disadvantaged. For his own security and peace of mind, this is an area he should not overlook.

As the Horse progresses through life, his earning capacity will improve and he will often be tempted to do more with his money, maybe travel further afield or spend more freely on others and his interests. But, while he will enjoy the pleasure his spending will bring, to be successful in money matters the Horse really should aim to build up some security for the longer term.

SUCCESS IN LOVE

Passionate, sensual and with so much to give, the Horse considers love highly important. He needs someone to love and to love him in return. He is not made for a solitary life and, with his often good looks, careful grooming and outgoing personality, he certainly knows how to attract – and also seduce.

The Horse falls in love easily and often at first sight. As with so many other aspects of his life, he likes things to happen quickly. When in love, his whole world can be transformed and he will go to great lengths to win and keep the love of another. Falling in love will be a rich, exciting and intoxicating experience for him, but sometimes he will find that what started off with such ardour and glory will not be long-lasting. The Horse will indeed experience several serious romances and find his love life does not always run smoothly. Although it may be difficult, especially when enjoying the intense passions of love, it could be in his interests to allow more time for a relationship to grow before entering into any commitment. At least this way he will give himself and his prospective partner chance to get to know each other better and so possibly put the relationship on a firmer foundation.

In choosing a partner, the Horse could find greatest happiness with someone with a similarly lively and adventurous spirit. He needs to keep active and to maintain his many interests and is certainly never one for a too restrictive or routine a lifestyle. Admittedly he can at times be self-centred and hot-tempered, and his partner needs to recognize that life with a Horse may not be necessarily smooth. But it can be a rich and wonderful experience, and when the Horse has the love and support he needs, he will be a devoted, loyal and generous partner.

SUCCESS AND OTHERS

The Horse is a keen socializer and enjoys being with others. With his wide interests and ability to speak so eloquently, he is highly regarded by many. However, as he prefers an active lifestyle as well as possesses a redoubtable nature, he will find his relations are significantly more rewarding with some signs than with others.

With a Rat

The Horse might, for a time, find the Rat a lively and sociable companion, but in the end their forthright and egoistical natures will get the better of them. Relations between them can be awkward.

In the parent–child relationship, the Horse parent will admire the Rat child's zeal and resourceful spirit, but could find it hard to build up a satisfactory rapport. Maybe it is due to their often different interests or self-willed personalities, but relations between them will need careful handling.

As colleagues, they may be keen and hard workers, but not together. The Horse will consider the Rat too much of an opportunist and too reliant on his wits and self-interest. Both are competitive and each will want to take the lead. With such a lack of trust and accord, they will often prefer to go their separate ways rather than struggle on together.

In love, with their lively and passionate natures these two could fall deeply for each other, but the way ahead could prove challenging. They are both strong-willed and each will want to dominate. The Horse, who so likes to maintain his own interests, could come to regard the Rat's meddling nature as inhibiting. With the Horse's temper and Rat's candidness there could be many stormy moments. A difficult match.

With an Ox

The Horse and Ox live life at different speeds and there will be little empathy between them.

In the parent–child relationship, the Horse parent will admire the Ox child's determined and methodical nature (the Horse is particularly respectful of those capable of standing their own ground), but their interests and outlooks do not really coincide and a certain closeness could be lacking.

As colleagues, the Horse is all for action while the Ox is steady and cautious. In time the Horse will come to view the Ox as an inhibiting influence and as both are so strong-willed, they will find it hard to reconcile their considerable differences.

In love, this will be a challenging match. Although the Horse may admire the loyalty and steadfastness of the Ox, he prefers a much more active lifestyle than the Ox is prepared to lead. With their different interests and outlooks, their relationship could soon become strained. Individually the Ox and Horse possess many great qualities, but they are not suited to each other.

With a Tiger

With both having such spirit and zest, the Horse and Tiger get on well together.

In the parent–child relationship, the Horse parent will admire the keen and enterprising ways of a Tiger child. There will be a good rapport between them and a close and enduring bond.

As colleagues, they make a dynamic duo. Both are action-oriented and together they will be forever testing ideas, pushing forward boundaries and setting themselves interesting goals. Provided they do not push themselves – or their luck – too far, these two have the drive and creativity to enjoy some worthy successes. An excellent combination.

In love, the Horse and Tiger are well suited. With their often similar interests and outlooks they understand each other well. Theirs will be a close relationship, with the Horse particularly admiring the Tiger's lively and supportive nature. These two signs are good for each other and their life together will be rewarding.

With a Rabbit

Although there are many qualities in the Rabbit that the Horse admires, their different natures and lifestyles do not always make for easy relations.

In the parent–child relationship, relations between a Horse parent and Rabbit child will need to be handled with care. The Rabbit child may be bright and keen, but desires a calm environment, something which may not always be possible with a lively, outgoing and volatile Horse in the household! Although the Horse parent will teach the young Rabbit well, relations will not always be comfortable.

As colleagues, their different attitudes will again lead to difficulties and they will not work well together. The Horse, always geared up for action, will find the more cautious approach of the Rabbit restrictive. Their general lack of accord does not bode well for any venture in which they become involved.

In love, the Rabbit and Horse can be deeply attracted to each other. They are both highly passionate signs and each will find in the other qualities they themselves may lack. The Horse will admire the Rabbit's calm nature and ordered existence, while the Rabbit will enjoy the Horse's vitality and zestful approach to life. But in essence, these two live their lives at different speeds and the Horse could find it hard to come to terms with the Rabbit's more sedate lifestyle. Their relationship may start well but turn into a challenging match.

With a Dragon

Being so outgoing and sociable, the Horse finds the Dragon interesting company and relations between them will generally be good.

In the parent–child relationship, the Horse parent will admire the resourceful and enterprising ways of the Dragon child. He will encourage the young Dragon and there will be a good understanding between them.

As colleagues, they both possess a determined streak and are keen to make the most of themselves. Each can learn from the other, with the Horse particularly appreciating the Dragon's enterprise and vision. Provided they remain united in their cause, then they can make a powerful and successful team.

In love, these two will enjoy life to the full. Energetic, outgoing and with so many shared interests, they can form a close and loving bond. The Horse will be particularly taken with the Dragon's sincere, confident and outgoing manner. Although both are assertive and frank in their views and there will be times when their forthright natures will clash, they will make a good match.

With a Snake

The Horse will realize there is more to the Snake than meets the eye and will be intrigued by this often complex and mysterious sign. In most situations, the Horse and Snake will get on reasonably well.

In the parent–child relationship, relations between the two signs will be at their most awkward. The Snake child is often quiet and reserved and could feel ill at ease with the energetic, dominant and highly charged style of a Horse parent, as well as wary of the Horse's short temper. These two will try, but there could be a lack of rapport between them.

As colleagues, the Horse and Snake can combine their strengths to good effect. The Horse will provide the impetus that the Snake needs to realize his potential, while the Snake will, through planning and advice, help the Horse to channel his considerable energies. Both will benefit and when united in a common goal, they make a good and often successful combination.

In love, these two will readily charm each other, both enchanted by the wonders of their rich and different personalities. The Horse will enjoy exploring the deep and thoughtful world of the Snake as well as appreciating his kindly and considerate manner. However, while their love can be strong and exciting, the Horse could come to resent the possessive nature and quieter lifestyle of the Snake. For their relationship to endure, adjustments will need to be made on both sides.

⤫ With another Horse

Sociable, active and outgoing, the Horse will find another of his sign a great companion. Relations between two Horses will be good.

In the parent–child relationship, there will be a close bond between parent and child. The Horse parent makes a good and wise teacher and he should aim to make the young Horse channel his energies in a focused way. The sooner the young Horse can learn self-discipline and control, the better his life will be.

As colleagues, two Horses will be earnest, hard-working and set on success, but there could be a constant jockeying for control and a certain rivalry between them. If they can agree on a division of responsibilities and stay focused on specific goal(s), however, then they can achieve a good degree of success.

In love, this will be a lively and passionate match. Both will be forever active, with a multitude of interests, an often busy social life and a love of travel. Amid all the activity, with their volatile natures and short tempers, there will be some stormy and difficult moments. But if they can ride these out, then theirs can be a special and exciting relationship.

⤫ With a Goat

The Horse likes the sociable and easy-going Goat and with many interests they can share, the two signs get on well.

In the parent–child relationship, the Horse parent will do much to build up the young Goat's confidence and self-esteem. There will be a good bond between them, although this will not be without the occasional rift, especially when the Horse feels the young Goat needs to put more effort into his activities or is too carefree in attitude, but generally their rapport is good.

As colleagues, they make an effective combination. Although the Horse will be keen to dominate, he will motivate the Goat and will appreciate the Goat's often creative approach. These two like each other and work well together, often with considerable success.

In love, the Horse and Goat make a good match. They understand and support each other and both will gain from their relationship. The Horse will particularly value the Goat's attentive and supportive manner as well as his input into home life. The genial Goat will also help to keep the Horse's more volatile side in check. Between them they will have many friends and when entertaining will make great hosts. Their relationship will be rich, meaningful and fun.

With a Monkey

The Horse may admire the lively nature of the Monkey but will not always feel entirely comfortable in his presence. Relations between them will be cool and reserved.

In the parent–child relationship, there will be times when Horse parent and Monkey child get on superbly well, particularly as they have interests they can share. However, there will also be times when the impish young Monkey will sorely test his parent's patience and, as he will soon discover, the Horse's patience is not strong!

As colleagues, the Horse and Monkey have the talents that *could* take them far. However, while the Horse may find the Monkey resourceful and enterprising, he will be suspicious of his ulterior motives as well as all too aware of his cunning streak. As a result there will be a lack of trust and accord between them and unless this can be addressed, these two will be forever undermining the success their combined talents could bring.

In love, this can prove a tricky match. The Horse may be taken with the Monkey's joyful and positive spirit and delight in sharing many interests with him, but both are strong-willed and each will want to prevail. The Horse may also be concerned by the Monkey's tendency to keep his thoughts and feelings to himself. It will take a special couple to make this relationship work.

With a Rooster

The Horse can find the Rooster lively and interesting company and for a time the pair may get on well. But once their forthright and self-willed natures come into play, problems will start.

In the parent–child relationship, the Horse parent will admire the young Rooster's keen, efficient and industrious nature, but the Rooster child is strong-willed and clashes with an equally redoubtable Horse parent are almost inevitable. They will admire each other, but their relations will not be easy.

As colleagues, they are both hard workers and can make a powerful combination. The Horse will particularly value the Rooster's fine organizational skills and ability to plan ahead. However, with both being egotists, each will be eager to claim the credit for the successes they will undoubtedly enjoy!

In love, they have much in common. Each likes to put on a show and together they can make a striking couple. They are both sociable and share many interests, including travel and the outdoors. In many ways they are well suited, but both are candid and can be stubborn and each will want to prevail, so there will be clashes and tricky moments. Provided they can adapt and work through any differences, however, theirs can be a fulfilling, albeit sometimes challenging match.

With a Dog

The Horse likes and understands the Dog and relations between them will be good.

In the parent–child relationship, the Horse parent can be a positive influence on the young Dog, building up his confidence, expanding his interests and bringing him out of his more despondent moments. The young Dog will respond well and love his Horse parent dearly.

As colleagues, these two complement each other and can make a successful team. They will respect each other and be mindful of each other's advice. The Horse will appreciate the Dog's steadying influence as well as his often shrewd judgement. Together these two can go far.

In love, the Horse and Dog are good for each other and can make a close and successful match. The Horse will especially appreciate the Dog's loyal, affectionate and supportive nature. They also have many interests in common, especially a liking for outdoor activities, and are highly compatible.

With a Pig

The Horse will be much taken with the Pig's genial, sociable and easy-going manner and relations between them will be good.

In the parent–child relationship, the Horse parent will admire the lively and good-natured Pig child and will have a great fondness for him. They will have interests they can share and the Pig child, so admiring of his outgoing Horse parent, will try hard to please. Admittedly both possess a stubborn streak, which can lead to some awkward moments, but in the main they will enjoy a close rapport.

As colleagues, they complement each other. The Horse will benefit from the Pig's more persistent and tenacious approach as well as recognize his considerable commercial talents. These two will often bring out the best in each other and by working closely together can enjoy a good level of success.

In love, the Horse and Pig seem made for each other. Their passion will be intense. Both are keen to enjoy life to the full and have so much to give. In addition to the strong physical attraction, they understand each other, with the Horse especially benefiting from the Pig's calmer and genial disposition. Should the Horse ever try to dominate, however, the Pig will resist in no uncertain terms! These two are well suited, though, and can make a successful match.

SUCCESS THROUGH LIFE

Active, enterprising and so keen to make his own way, the Horse has the abilities to make much of his life and his progress will be both eventful and varied. He has wide interests and works hard, and once he has found his calling in life, he can enjoy a good level of success. However, first he will need to conquer his restless spirit.

In his childhood years, the young Horse will delight in finding out about all manner of things and will be active and adventurous. He will have a lively and sometimes mischievous streak and be quick to learn. However, he also desires a certain independence and is never one to be restricted or bound by countless rules and regulations. This will inevitably lead to clashes with those around him and without sufficient discipline and guidance, the young Horse's wilful streak could well lead to difficulties, both in childhood and in later life. As with the animal, the young Horse needs good training.

The Horse will often leave home at an early age, eager to taste the freedom adult life can bring. In his work he will be keen to try many different types of job, while on a personal level, many Horses choose to marry young or quickly settle down with a partner. The Horse's life in his late teens and early twenties can be a fascinating and joyous time. However, as the years pass and responsibilities mount, strains can start to appear. Sometimes a relationship formed too hastily could flounder and the Horse could feel his career lacks direction and that he is not making as much progress as he would wish. It is in their mid to late twenties that many Horses will learn some hard truths about life and will need to make a real effort to curb their restless tendencies.

As the Horse enters middle age, he will generally become more settled and happier in himself. Often with family responsibilities and his career on track, he will be better able to realize his potential and will often enjoy a good measure of success. A resulting improvement in his financial situation will also give him more chance to indulge in his various interests, including his love of travel, so making this period of his life a pleasant and fulfilling time.

In old age, too, the Horse will continue to draw much satisfaction from his various interests as well as enjoy the companionship of his friends and loved ones. His later years will again be a time of much personal satisfaction.

As the Horse has such an active and keen spirit, his life will certainly be eventful. While the first stages will sometimes be challenging and unsettled, once the Horse has mastered his impulsive and restless nature he will find life becoming more meaningful and successful.

FAMOUS HORSES

Neil Armstrong, Rowan Atkinson, P. T. Barnum, Samuel Beckett, Ingmar Bergman, Leonard Bernstein, Ray Charles, Chopin, Sir Sean Connery, Billy Connolly, Catherine Cookson, Kevin Costner, James Dean, Clint Eastwood, Thomas Alva Edison, Harrison Ford, Aretha Franklin, Sir Bob Geldof, Samuel Goldwyn, Billy Graham, Gene Hackman, Rita Hayworth, Jimi Hendrix, Aldous Huxley, Calvin Klein, Lenin, Annie Lennox, Desmond Lynam, Sir Paul McCartney, Nelson Mandela, Princess Margaret, Spike Milligan, Ben Murphy, Sir Isaac Newton, Louis Pasteur, Puccini, Rembrandt, Jean Renoir, Anita Roddick, Theodore Roosevelt, Helena Rubenstein, Alexander Solzhenitsyn, Barbra Streisand, John Travolta, Kathleen Turner, Mike Tyson, Vivaldi, Robert Wagner, Billy Wilder, Andy Williams, the Duke of Windsor, Boris Yeltsin.

SUCCESS TIPS FOR THE HORSE

The Horse has a restless side to his nature and his quest for new experiences or the attraction of new temptations may lead him to abandon a great deal. Sometimes his actions can be too hasty and he can make decisions without thinking of the consequences. In so much of his life, the Horse needs to think his actions through and to plan ahead. That way he will find his life becoming more purposeful as well as sometimes being able to prevent the mistakes that impulsive and hot-headed action can bring.

The Horse is a very outgoing person, but while he is so effective in putting himself across, he is not always that good a listener. In some instances, rather than being so keen to impress others with his own viewpoint, he needs to consider those of others. Sometimes he can be narrow-minded and there will be times when he would benefit from actively seeking and *listening* to the advice of others. So many think so highly of him that he should profit from their wisdom.

Also, the Horse is good at generating ideas, but he does not always make the most of them and in some instances he does need the help of others in their realization. Rather than let his ideas come to nothing, the Horse should seek help and again listen to the advice he is given. The Horse is a creator, but to succeed he does so often need the assistance and encouragement of others.

The Horse would also do well to learn the value of persistence. Sometimes fear of failure will cause him to change course or obstacles will make him give up all too easily. However, it is through dealing with difficulties that so much can be learnt. It is at these times that new strengths can be discovered, new ideas emerge and vital experience be gained. Particularly in work matters, the Horse should have more faith in himself and persist with his dreams *even when the going gets tough*. It is the persistent who so often are the triumphant.

The Horse likes to live fast and does not have a patient nature. However, in order to advance and to realize potential it *is* necessary to prepare for the longer term. Sometimes results do take a long time to achieve and the Horse should allow for this. He has the abilities and personality to do well, but to succeed he needs time to develop, to build up experience and to find his niche. He should take the time and should look ahead more. The rewards that life can bring need to be worked for.

SOME FINAL THOUGHTS FROM HORSES

Your success depends on what you do yourself, with your own means.

P. T. Barnum

Experience is not what happens to a man. It is what a man does with what happens to him.

Aldous Huxley

If you do things well, do them better. Be daring, be different, be just.

Anita Roddick

The three great essentials to achieve anything worthwhile are, first, hard work; second, stick-to-itiveness; third, common sense.

Thomas Alva Edison

Many of life's failures are people who did not realize how close they were to success when they gave up.

Thomas Alva Edison

Do what you can, with what you have, where you are.

Theodore Roosevelt

No man needs sympathy because he has to work... Far and away the best prize that life offers is the chance to work hard at work worth doing.

Theodore Roosevelt

It is only through labour and painful effort, by grim energy and resolute courage, that we move on to better things.
Theodore Roosevelt

These three things – work, will, success – fill human existence. Will opens the door to success, both brilliant and happy, work passes these doors, and at the end of the journey success comes in to crown one's efforts.
Louis Pasteur

The
Goat

Whether grazing in lush green fields or living in more mountainous terrain, there is an air of contentment about the Goat. Unless troubled by some threat – when he is capable of nimbly getting out of the way or of kicking out with some force – the Goat will lead a peaceable existence, feeling secure in his home surroundings. He knows what is good for him and he does enjoy life. And so do many born under the eighth and most feminine of the Chinese signs.

The Goat has an easy-going nature. He is quiet, amiable and gets on well with others. He also possesses a delicious sense of fun and his humour and easy manner make him popular company. A keen socializer, he will have a wide circle of friends and is particularly admired for his discretion and understanding. He tends to come into his own at social gatherings and not only will he make the most of these but he can also be a most thoughtful and attentive host. With his good manners, charm and convivial nature, the Goat really does have the happy knack of making others comfortable in his presence.

The Goat is, however, greatly influenced by his surroundings. Being a gentle soul, he does not like discord or a particularly pressured atmosphere. In some cases, he will even turn a blind eye to difficult situations so that he can remain unaffected by them. He is all for a pleasant and settled existence and in this he can be relatively successful. Throughout his life the Goat will enjoy a reasonable level of good fortune and often have the means to live in comfort.

However, while the Goat can certainly lead a contented and successful life (success to him so often meaning security and stability), he does possess traits which could prevent him from achieving all he might. One of his chief weaknesses is his indecisiveness. The Goat agonizes long and hard over decisions and will often wish others could take them for him or that events would unfold in such a way as to render a decision unnecessary. Not only can his indecision exasperate those around him, but it could also result in him missing opportunities while he makes his mind up.

Allied to this, the Goat does not like taking the initiative. He is more of a follower than a leader and his reticence in taking action or in not following his ideas through can again undermine his level of success. Although no one welcomes the threat of failure and rejection, to get on in life it *is* necessary to push forward and to take risks – and sometimes be hurt in the process. The Goat must accept this and he owes it both to himself and those who have so much faith in him to be more assertive and to make the most of his considerable abilities. Rather than dwell on what might go wrong – and the Goat does have a pessimistic streak – or worry too much over what others may be thinking, he should set about his activities with greater determination. With his ability to think so imaginatively, to generate ideas and to get on so well with others, he really does have a lot in his favour and he should make the most of it.

The Goat is the most artistically gifted of all the Chinese signs. Whether through creative expression or appreciating beauty, he has talent and taste. In his work he will often find that he does well in positions which allow him to tap into his creativity. Unlike some signs, who may be driven by more material considerations, the Goat's reward is to find fulfilment and pleasure in what he does. And to be appreciated.

The Goat also has a fondness for the countryside and whenever possible will try to live away from the bustle and frenzy of cities in smaller communities, preferably where he can be close to family and friends. Indeed, the family is another very important element to the Goat's life and while he will often leave the parental home at an early age, he will always maintain close links with his parents. Family bonds are important to him.

The Goat will also try to imbue his own home life with a close and congenial atmosphere, free from the discord which he so hates. He will take great care in the setting up of his home and with his fine artistic taste, it will often be full of *objets d'art*, knick-knacks and exquisite and sometimes unusual souvenirs that he has acquired over the years. The Goat may not be particularly well organized or neat, but in his home he will know where everything is as well as maintain a high standard of cleanliness. The Goat's home will certainly be stamped with his personality – a happy and carefree place with a charm very much its own.

As the Goat has such a sociable nature, he will rarely be short of admirers. However, his love life will not be the smoothest. The Goat can experience difficulty in expressing his feelings and, not wishing to hurt others or be involved in unpleasantness should things not be working out, he can let relationships drift or find himself in situations which are not always ideal. In his dealings with others, the Goat needs to be more forthcoming about how he really feels rather than being evasive or so diplomatic that his true feelings remain concealed. However, while his love life will bring moments of anxiety, the

Goat usually chooses his partner well. Ideally this will be someone who is similarly loving and attentive but also supportive. Throughout his life, the Goat does so need someone to turn to, to confide in, depend upon and love. In return, he makes a caring and affectionate partner. If he becomes a parent, he will love and care deeply for his children and while his easy-going manner makes him no disciplinarian, he will often enjoy a close rapport with them.

The male Goat is genial, easy to get on with and possesses a rich humour. While he may be annoyingly indecisive at times and cares a great deal about what others think, he does possess a creative and original mind and once inspired can make a real impression. He is very much a family man and is particularly thoughtful towards his loved ones. In appearance he can be smart when the occasion calls for it, but he tends to prefer more casual clothes in keeping with his easy-going nature.

The female Goat also chooses her clothes with great care, picking those which show her to her best advantage. Whether dressed in dainty, skimpy or flowing clothing, she is attractive and often elegant. She is attentive over her general appearance as well and has a skilful way with both her make-up and her hair. In her manner, the female Goat is warm and friendly and makes great company. She may not be the most organized or punctual of people, but she has a good heart and is caring towards others. Her joy in life is her family and home life and here her talents for creating a settled and loving atmosphere are supreme.

The Goat takes great pleasure in maintaining a variety of interests, so keeping the different aspects of his life in some sort of balance. Again his artistic and creative talents will be to the fore and whether he is attracted to craftwork, art, music, writing, photography or some other form of expression, his interests can be a rewarding part of his life. He can also enjoy going to the theatre, cinema or concerts as well as visiting places of interest.

With his concern for the environment, the Goat can also be a keen recycler and whether inventing new uses for old items or using discarded items, his ingenuity and creativity will impress others. Another of his interests is shopping, including window-shopping.

The Goat may prefer to live life at a gentler pace than some and is certainly not the most ambitious or thrusting. But while his life may sometimes lack drama, his good luck, abilities and amiable nature will serve him well. Those Goats who are born on a rainy day are considered to have the most luck, but all Goats do have the personality, the talents and charm to lead a contented and rewarding life.

SUCCESS AND WORK

The Goat much prefers working as part of a team to working on his own. Not only is he more comfortable with colleagues around to liaise with, but being part of a group also gives him a greater sense of direction and more security – and he can leave the decision-making to others while he gets on with his own duties.

The Goat is a careful worker. He likes to get things right and sometimes can be fussy over the smallest of details. Should things go wrong, he will take it (and any criticism) very much to heart. He has a creative mind and is capable of producing some fine ideas. However, to really thrive, the Goat needs to feel that he has the support of others. Again being part of a group can help, but very often the Goat will really benefit from having a mentor, someone who can provide support and guidance and help him bring his talents to the fore. Indeed, many successful Goats have benefited from the support and encouragement of another. In turn those Goats who do take on positions of power and responsibility, while not always relishing their role, will show themselves to be fair-minded and responsible and, because of their decent and personable nature, will win the respect of many.

As far as possible the Goat should avoid positions of too routine a nature, where his freedom of expression will be stifled, or those in too pressurized an environment. The cut and thrust of quick decision-making or fierce commercial competition does not suit the Goat's style or temperament. He prefers stability and a structure to his work.

Goats are happiest when they are allowed to express themselves and able to draw on their creative gifts. As a profession, this can take many forms, but if he is involved in writing, music, art or the performing arts, the Goat can make an impact. Also, with his eye for detail and artistic flair, he can do well as a designer, architect, illustrator or arranger, whether for an exhibition, museum, shop window or website. With his sense of style, as well as ability to work so well with others, he could also enjoy success as a hairdresser or in the fashion industry or interior design.

To be a success and find fulfilment, the Goat does not necessarily have to be at the forefront of activity. Instead he is content to work at what he does best in the knowledge that it is appreciated. Provided he feels comfortable with his situation and has the support of those around him, then he can make a valuable contribution in whichever career he chooses.

SUCCESS AND MONEY

The Goat enjoys a reasonable amount of good fortune in money matters and whether through his own efforts, the support of a partner, an inheritance or a stroke of luck, he almost always has the means to enjoy a comfortable lifestyle. And he does so like to live well.

However, the Goat is a spendthrift. Whether buying something for himself or his loved ones or acquiring yet more items for his home, he loves to shop. He also has a generous streak and will spend quite freely when out socializing. However, he can be over-trusting and there is a risk that some might take advantage of his good nature. In some situations, the Goat should be more discerning.

Similarly, he should take tighter control over his purse strings. Sometimes he does spend all too readily – and unnecessarily. He should reflect more on his purchases and not always be in such a great hurry to spend any surplus cash he may have. Although it may seem a lot less fun, he should aim to manage his money, perhaps setting up a regular savings account as well as setting sums aside for specific requirements, whether for his home, transport, a holiday or some other purpose. With greater control and planning, the Goat will find his finances becoming more secure as well as easier to manage.

Also, when making any major purchase or investment, the Goat would always do well to check the details and any obligations he is taking on. Without care, his lack of interest in the small print can be costly. In money matters, the Goat's generally laid-back and trusting manner can leave him vulnerable as well as misled.

Although Goats are generally not interested in the intricacies of high finance or strongly motivated by commercial gain, they do enjoy money, as it enables them to spend and to live in style. While the Goat does often have a happy knack of attracting money, or at least the means to tide himself over, he should aim to take a greater control over the financial side of his life, preserving, protecting and making the most of his assets.

SUCCESS AND LOVE

The Goat has a caring heart and he yearns for someone who will be loyal, dependable and supportive. While his quest for true love may not always be smooth, once he has found a soulmate, he will be truly content. Love and life in a supportive and agreeable atmosphere are just so important to the Goat. However, to get to this happy state will require some effort.

In his search for love, the Goat will go through periods of considerable personal anguish. Sometimes he has difficulty in expressing his *true* feelings, ever aware of the effect his words will have on another. So unsatisfactory relationships can drift or the Goat can build up too much hope in the early stages of courtship. Sometimes he tries too hard to find love, rather than letting it happen by chance, as it so often does.

There will be times, certainly in the Goat's late teens, when he will be hurt and suffer much anxiety, but his desire for love – real love – will triumph and many Goats will eventually find an ideal partner, someone confident in manner, willing to support the Goat in his interests and activities, and also fairly tolerant. They will need to be prepared to understand the Goat's foibles and swings in mood as well as enjoy his sometimes whimsical nature. Once that person has won the heart of the Goat, then they will have gained a partner who is caring, affectionate and attentive, and who will pour much energy into establishing what will be a settled and agreeable home life.

SUCCESS WITH OTHERS

With his friendly and easy-going nature, the Goat gets on well with many. However, being so aware of the feelings of others, he will find there are certain signs he is able to be more comfortable with than others.

With a Rat

Although the Goat may for a time find the Rat lively and interesting company, these two do not really understand each other and relations between them are rarely good.

In the parent–child relationship, relations between Goat parent and Rat child will need careful handling. Although the Goat parent will love his resourceful Rat child dearly, the young Rat is often a bundle of energy and his boisterous and adventurous ways will not always find favour with the Goat, who wants a peaceful existence!

As colleagues, the Goat and Rat do not work well together. In particular, the Goat does not have the opportunism or commercial instincts of the Rat and could feel uncomfortable with the constant bustle and activity that a Rat colleague generates. To do well the Goat needs someone more on his own wavelength, someone he can build up a rapport with. The Rat is not that person.

In love, the Goat and Rat are both romantic and passionate signs and with their genial and sociable natures, they could find themselves attracted to each other. Unfortunately the prospects do not tend to be good and their personalities will invariably clash. The Goat will not like the forthright and candid nature of the Rat or his rather thrifty attitude towards money. He could come to regard him as impatient and unsympathetic. A difficult match.

With an Ox

Although there will be qualities that the Goat admires in the Ox – and sometimes wishes he possessed – their interests and personalities are so very different that relations between them will be poor.

In the parent–child relationship, the interests and attitudes of a Goat parent and Ox child do not always coincide. The young Ox likes order and routine and may not always appreciate his Goat parent's more capricious nature. These two will try, and the Goat parent will admire the young Ox's dutiful manner, but their rapport will not always be the strongest.

As colleagues, difficulties will loom. While the Goat will value working with someone who is both resolute and prepared to take the lead, he could find the Ox just too overpowering. The Ox may have drive and commitment, but he can also be obstinate, intransigent and impatient, none of which will endear him to the Goat. These two will irritate each other and prefer to go their separate ways.

In love, this will be a difficult match. Admittedly the Goat may seek a robust and strong-willed partner, but the Ox does not possess the patience or tolerance the Goat needs. The Goat delights in a carefree, easy-going existence, while the Ox is all for planning and routine. Also, being so sensitive, the Goat will not appreciate the Ox's forthright nature. There is indeed a wide gulf between them and it will take a special couple to bridge it.

With a Tiger

The Goat admires the sincere, good-hearted and lively Tiger and relations between the two signs are often good.

In the parent–child relationship, relations could be at their most awkward. The Goat parent is not disciplinarian and could find the headstrong and sometimes boisterous Tiger child a trial. However, with care and time spent on interests they can both enjoy, relations could be improved and a greater understanding arise.

As colleagues, both are innovators and between them will have a fund of ideas. Each will respect and support the other, with the Goat drawing strength from the Tiger's enterprising and enthusiastic nature. However, while they can do well together, with their extravagant tendencies, they would do well to hire a good financial adviser!

In love, the Goat and Tiger are well suited. They are both keen socializers and have creative and imaginative natures. They will have many interests to share and enjoy. The Goat will be particularly reassured by having such a loyal, honourable and protective partner. There will be a good understanding between them and they make a good match.

✃ With a Rabbit

The Goat has a great liking and respect for the quiet and genial Rabbit and relations between the two signs are often excellent.

In the parent–child relationship, the Goat parent and Rabbit child will enjoy a particularly close understanding. The Goat will provide the love, care and support that the young Rabbit so needs in order to flourish and with their fondness for the arts and creative pursuits, they will have many interests they can share. There will be a great bond between them.

As colleagues, the Goat and Rabbit work well together, with a good level of trust. The Goat will especially value the Rabbit's temperament, judgement and good business sense. Together they can make a successful team, especially if their work allows them to make the most of their ideas and creative talents.

In love, the Goat and Rabbit are ideally suited and can find much happiness together. Both are genial and peace-loving signs wanting nothing more than a secure, comfortable and stable existence. With such similar interests and outlooks, and each being so supportive of the other, theirs will be a blissful relationship.

With a Dragon

The Goat will enjoy the Dragon's dynamic and sparkling company, but after a time, when the differences in their natures become apparent, relations could cool.

In the parent–child relationship, the Goat parent will be proud of the resourcefulness and talents of the Dragon child, although the young Dragon's strong will and sometimes rebellious nature will cause him much anxiety. Nevertheless, there will be much love between them.

As colleagues, the Goat will find the Dragon an often inspirational colleague and supportive influence. There will be a good understanding between the two and when working towards a specific goal, they can achieve a great deal.

In love, there will be passion, excitement and fun. With their outgoing and sociable natures, there will be so much for these two to enjoy. The Goat will particularly value having such a dependable, confident and lively partner. But the longer term could be tricky, with the Goat finding the Dragon's restless and impulsive nature an unsettling influence. For the relationship to succeed, there will need to be a great deal of understanding on both sides.

With a Snake

The Goat has a great fondness for the quiet, reflective and often amusing Snake and relations between the two signs can be good.

In the parent–child relationship, the Goat parent will do much to encourage the young Snake and help him to become more outwardly confident, and the Snake child will respond well. There will be a good bond between them.

As colleagues, the Goat and Snake work well together, with the Goat admiring the careful and considered ways of the

Snake. There will be a good rapport and respect between them and, if their work allows them to combine their ideas and creative talents, then they could be on course for great success. And when it comes, they will certainly enjoy it in style!

In love, the Goat and Snake make a good match. Quiet and peaceable, with a fondness for the finer things in life, they have much in common. The Goat will draw strength from the Snake's kindly and supportive ways and even temperament. Both seek a secure and settled existence and they can find much happiness together.

With a Horse

With many interests in common, the Goat gets on well with the Horse and relations between the two signs are good.

In the parent–child relationship, the independent and self-willed nature of the Horse child will sometimes prove a trial for the Goat parent, but despite some difficult moments, with interests and activities to share and enjoy, there will be considerable affection between them.

As colleagues, they can make a successful team. Each will support and encourage the other and they will combine their different strengths to good effect, with the Goat admiring the Horse's industrious nature as well as finding him an often inspirational figure. These two like and respect each other and together can enjoy a good level of success.

In love, the Goat and Horse are well suited. They are good for each other, with the Goat benefiting from the Horse's confident and positive manner as well as valuing his affectionate nature. With their similar tastes and interests, their life together can be rich, rewarding and interesting. These two can find much happiness.

≤ With another Goat

Goats know how to enjoy themselves and two Goats together will get on very well indeed.

In the parent–child relationship, there will be a great love and affinity between Goat parent and Goat child. Both are kindly and affectionate and the young Goat will strive to please his parent. The bond will be made all the stronger because they will enjoy so many similar interests.

As colleagues, these two like and respect each other and, with their creative natures, are capable of generating some brilliant ideas. They will inspire and motivate each other and could enjoy considerable success. However, as the Goat is not the most commercially-minded of signs, two Goats would do well to work closely with a suitable adviser and accountant.

In love, with their passionate, amorous and easy-going natures, two Goats are well suited. They will lavish love and attention on their home as well as have a fond appreciation of the good things in life. Goats do like to spend, but provided their finances hold, theirs will be a close, harmonious and often happy relationship.

≤ With a Monkey

The Goat thinks well of the lively and resourceful Monkey and relations between the two signs are good.

In the parent–child relationship, there will be a close bond between a Goat parent and Monkey child. The Goat parent will do much to encourage the young Monkey's inquisitive and imaginative nature and with their generally spirited approach, both will enjoy a fine rapport.

As colleagues, the Goat and Monkey work well together, with the Goat appreciating the Monkey's resourcefulness and commercial acumen. There will be a good understanding between them and their often inventive and sometimes unconventional approach can lead them to considerable success.

In love, the Goat and Monkey are often attracted to each other. Each is easy-going and there will be much fun and variety in their relationship. They enjoy each other's qualities, with the Goat especially valuing the good-natured and companionable ways of the Monkey. There will be a good rapport between them and they can make a loving couple.

With a Rooster

With their different temperaments and outlooks, relations between these two signs are poor.

In the parent–child relationship, the Goat parent may admire the Rooster child's efficient and industrious nature, but with a mind of his own and a sometimes demanding nature, the young Rooster could give the Goat some difficult times. Both will try, but relations between them will need care.

As colleagues, the Goat and Rooster have different attitudes and styles and, while the Goat may admire the Rooster's organizational skills, he will find him fussy, candid and an exacting task master. Unless both are particularly inspired by their work and can combine their talents, the lack of accord between them will not lead to a successful working relationship.

In love, each can learn from the other, with the Goat often benefiting from the Rooster's more methodical and orderly nature. They also have some mutual interests, including a love of nature. But their personalities are very different and the Goat will often be unsettled by the Rooster's candid and matter-of-fact manner. For the relationship to succeed, there will need to be considerable adjustments and great tolerance on both sides. Not an easy relationship.

With a Dog

With their different personalities and few interests in common, there is little accord between the Goat and Dog.

In the parent–child relationship, both the Goat parent and Dog child have kindly and affectionate natures and at times there will be a close bond between them. However, the young Dog can be stubborn and temperamental and the Goat parent capricious, and there will be occasions when their relationship will need careful handling.

As colleagues, both are worriers and both like to have a sense of direction, yet as neither will feel at ease with the other, with the Dog being more idealistic and less imaginative than the Goat, they do not gel. As a result, their working relationship will not be good.

In love, the Goat and Dog could find the way ahead challenging. Although the Goat may value the Dog's affectionate nature, they could find it difficult to build up a satisfactory rapport. The Dog is direct, practical and matter of fact, while the Goat is more laid-back and casual. Both can be worriers and together could become quite melancholy. Individually they have wonderful qualities, but they do not understand each other.

With a Pig

Both genial and good-natured with an appreciation of the good life, the Goat and Pig enjoy each other's company and relations between them are often excellent.

In the parent–child relationship, the affectionate Pig child will respond well to the loving ways of the Goat parent and there will be a close bond between them. The keen Pig child will do much to please his Goat parent.

As colleagues, their often different talents and skills complement each other and together they make a successful team. The

Goat will particularly benefit from the Pig's commercial flair as well as from having such a robust, supportive and agreeable colleague. These two could enjoy considerable success together.

In love, the Goat and Pig can make a close and loving match. Both are easy-going and desire a settled and harmonious existence. And with their fun-loving, sociable and passionate natures, plus the many interests they enjoy, there will be a good understanding between them. Both also like to live in style. They are well suited.

SUCCESS THROUGH LIFE

Peace-loving, genial and with a kindly nature, the Goat is well regarded and throughout his life will enjoy the support of many. People do warm to him and want to help him and as a consequence he will enjoy good fortune. Throughout his years the Goat will rarely lack for basic comforts and will often enjoy a good lifestyle.

As a child, the Goat is particularly sensitive to his surroundings and needs a secure and stable environment in which to grow. He needs to feel loved and supported and in return will do his utmost to please those who mean so much to him. Admittedly there will be times when he finds the world hostile, or when problems at school, perhaps criticism or bad marks, will knock his confidence. It is at such times that the Goat needs support and to be shown how to deal with more demanding situations. Despite these difficult moments, the young Goat will be popular with his peers as well as enjoying creative and imaginative games and hobbies. His childhood years can be content, although so much does depend on the Goat's home situation. Should this be unstable or difficult, then the Goat's world and outlook will be deeply affected.

As he enters adulthood, the Goat will often be keen to find a partner as well as develop his own talents. This can be an exciting, although sometimes daunting time. But often the Goat's luck will hold and after several romances, he will find his ideal partner as well as obtain a job which will be a satisfying outlet for his talents. It is also at this time he will devote much energy into setting up his own home, one which has style and ambience.

Should he become a parent, the Goat will devote much time and energy to the welfare and upbringing of his children. In addition to showering them with love – and often spoiling them – he will do a lot to encourage their creative spirits. This can be a wonderful stage in the Goat's life.

As the Goat enters middle age, his experiences will have led him to become more assertive and confident, and in his work, having found his true *métier*, he can look forward to making good progress. How great this is does, though, depend upon the Goat's degree of ambition. There will be many Goats who will be content to stay in the same role for many years. The Goat's family and social life will, as ever, remain so important to him. However when his children enter their teenage years and start to exercise their independence, the Goat could go through some worrying periods.

The Goat's old age will, though, be an often contented stage for him as he fondly watches the progress of the various members of his family as well as in many cases enjoying the pleasures of being a grandparent.

Admittedly, life always throws up problems and delivers some blows and at times the sensitive Goat will suffer deeply and feel that the world is closing in on him. But with the support and love of another, he will recover and often learn much in the process. And with his many interests, his talents and his personable nature, he can indeed lead an agreeable and satisfying life, and so often in the style that he wants.

FAMOUS GOATS

Pamela Anderson, Jane Austen, Cilla Black, Lord Byron, Leslie Caron, John le Carré, Miguel de Cervantes, Coco Chanel, Nat 'King' Cole, Catherine Deneuve, Charles Dickens, Ken Dodd, Sir Arthur Conan Doyle, Daphne Du Maurier, Douglas Fairbanks, Dame Margot Fonteyn, Bill Gates, Mel Gibson, Whoopi Goldberg, Mikhail Gorbachev, John Grisham, Oscar Hammerstein II, George Harrison, Sir Edmund Hillary, Julio Iglesias, Mick Jagger, Buster Keaton, Nicole Kidman, Ben Kingsley, Franz Liszt, John Major, Michelangelo, Joni Mitchell, Rupert Murdoch, Robert de Niro, Michael Palin, Eva Peron, Marcel Proust, Keith Richards, Julia Roberts, Richard Brinsley Sheridan, Jerry Springer, William Makepeace Thackeray, Lana Turner, Mark Twain, Rudolph Valentino, Barbara Walters, John Wayne, Bruce Willis.

SUCCESS TIPS FOR THE GOAT

The Goat possesses a sensitive nature and is keenly aware of the views and feelings of others. Sometimes, concerned about the reaction he may get, he holds back from taking action or making the most of himself. At times he can be too easily influenced. To get results and realize his potential, the Goat should aim to stand his ground more often and do what *he* wants. He is the master of his own destiny and he needs to take control of it. By becoming more resolute and doing what he in his own heart wants to do, he can make his life more fulfilling and successful.

It is true that in work, especially when promoting ideas and going after opportunities, some failures and setbacks are inevitable. Although these can be so hard and seem so unfair, it is often at such times that one is able to grow and develop strength. The Goat should remember this and after setbacks he should keep faith with himself and not give up. It is by persisting that success will ultimately come. As the Chinese proverb states, 'If you get up one more time than you fall, you will make it through.'

The Goat reflects a great deal and very often his thoughts tend towards the negative, leading him to become anxious and pessimistic about certain situations. This can have an adverse effect upon his whole bearing. When the Goat finds himself indulging in negative thinking, he should try to steer his thoughts towards something more positive and uplifting. We do, after all, choose what we think about and by thinking of past successes rather than failures, happier moments rather than sad, and positive emotions rather than fears and doubts, the Goat will find his thoughts give him strength rather than have a weakening effect. To be successful, the Goat needs to direct his energies towards the positive. As Charles Dickens, himself a Goat, wrote, 'Reflect upon your present blessings, of which every man has many; not on your past misfortune, of which all men have some.'

Also, despite his best intentions, the Goat is not the most methodical of people. Some Goats are untidy and some fail to plan or organize their activities well. All this can be to the Goat's detriment. If he finds he is not making the most of himself or his time or appears to be floundering, he could be helped by mounting an efficiency drive and aiming to get on top of his situation. The more methodical and ordered he can be, the more he can achieve.

If the Goat has a particular talent that he wishes to nurture or a career he wants to follow, then he should take positive steps towards realizing his aim. One step which he would do well to consider is to contact those able to give him *informed* advice.

The aspiring writer, musician or artist, for instance, rather than seeking the inexperienced views of a friend, should be bold and seek the views of a professional. In many cases, he will greatly benefit from what he is told and some Goats may find that someone they approach will take an interest in their progress or be someone they can emulate. Many Goats have gone on to some great achievements thanks to the support of a inspirational figure and the Goat should make sure he has such a figure.

SOME FINAL THOUGHTS FROM GOATS

If you don't have a dream, how are you going to make a dream come true?
Oscar Hammerstein II

The world is a looking glass and gives back to every man the reflection of his own face. Frown at it and it will in turn look sourly upon you; laugh at it and with it, and it is a jolly, kind companion.
William Makepeace Thackeray

Diligence is the mother of good fortune.
Miguel de Cervantes

The real voyage of discovery consists not in seeking new landscapes, but in having new eyes.
Marcel Proust

Always do right; this will gratify some people and astonish the rest.
Mark Twain

Keep away from people who try to belittle your ambitions. Small people always do that. But the really great make you feel that you too can become great.
Mark Twain

Twenty years from now you will be more disappointed by the things that you didn't do than by the ones you did do. So throw off the bowlines. Sail away from the safe harbour. Catch the trade winds in your sails. Explore. Dream. Discover.
Mark Twain

The surest way not to fail is to determine to succeed.
Richard Brinsley Sheridan

The
Monkey

Whether playing chase, swinging through the trees or rolling around on the ground, there is a great sense of fun about the Monkey. He enjoys life and his keen and often lively nature is so often found in those born under the ninth Chinese sign.

The Monkey is a quick thinker and is always alert. He never likes to miss what is going on and has an inquisitive and enquiring mind. He also has a good memory and is able to impress others with his swift recall. In addition, the Monkey is an excellent communicator. With his charm and his ability to take in details, he can be a persuasive and interesting as well as sometimes witty speaker. The Monkey certainly knows how to impress and makes popular and agreeable company.

The Monkey likes to keep himself active. If there is something he wants done, he will not sit for lengthy periods drawing out detailed plans or procrastinating. He is very much geared up for swift action. Similarly, when he has ideas he wishes to try out, there will be no holding him back. Sometimes his haste can lead to less satisfactory results, but at least the Monkey will know he has given his idea a try. There is no 'What if?' about the Monkey. His philosophy is 'Let's give it a go and see what happens.' He is also particularly adept at sorting out problems and coming up with the most ingenious of solutions.

Both talented and original, the Monkey truly has a great deal in his favour and by channelling his energies well is capable of achieving considerable success in life. But he also has his failings and these he should watch. In some instances, the Monkey reduces his levels of success by spreading his energies too widely. Ever curious and wanting to be involved, he can sometimes be committed to so much that it can prevent him from concentrating on specific goals and objectives. He can get distracted easily, too, and again a more focused and discipline approach would certainly help. In addition, the Monkey does like swift results, but sometimes the road to success can be a lengthy one and the Monkey must accept this and not give up or get distracted too easily.

The Monkey is highly self-reliant. He likes to be in control of his own destiny. But in his eagerness to succeed, he can resort to methods which may not always enhance his reputation. The Monkey can be cunning and devious, and while in some cases this can bring him some gain, those around him may start to become wary and suspicious of him and he could lose support as a result. If he resorts to such tactics, the Monkey should be prepared to take the consequences! There will also be occasions when he tries to overreach himself and push his luck just a little too far.

Also, due to the strong faith he has in his abilities, the Monkey does tend to possess a superiority complex. Although he conceals this well, his certainty that he knows best can stop him from consulting others and benefiting from their advice. The Monkey is undeniably talented, but he must not close his mind to the help that others could give, if only he would let them.

Like us all, the Monkey does have his faults, but he is so genial, good humoured and artful that he is often able to get away with a great deal. To some he may seem a rascal or likeable rogue, but life would certainly be less fun without his presence.

The Monkey is born under the sign of fantasy and he does possess a fertile imagination. He is creative and enterprising. However, there will be occasions when he does get carried away with his thoughts and in his excitement exaggerates or forgets certain practicalities. But even if some of the ideas the Monkey puts forward may not be possible, at least he is always driving forward and always keen. And if something does not work out, then he is more than capable of turning his attention to something else. The Monkey's resourcefulness will keep him going and so often he will win through in the end.

Being so inquisitive and versatile, the Monkey could find his work and interests taking him in many directions. Whatever he chooses to do, he will set about his activities with enthusiasm and originality. Provided he remains focused, rather than always jumping from one activity to another, then he certainly has it within him to achieve a good level of success.

As far as his personal interests are concerned, the Monkey often enjoys mentally stimulating activities and could be particularly enthusiastic about chess or other strategic-type games, crosswords and word puzzles. He also likes practical activities and could derive much satisfaction from carrying out projects on his home or in some form of craftwork. The Monkey also has a fondness for music and could enjoy playing an instrument or singing. He is also an insatiable reader and a keen traveller. He likes company and whether meeting up for a chat, partying or just going out somewhere, the Monkey enjoys socializing.

However, while the Monkey does get on well with others and will have many friends and acquaintances, his love life is not always so easy. He certainly knows how to ingratiate himself with others and how to attract, but he holds back from expressing his true feelings. A lot of the Monkey is for show, but there is a strictly personal side to him which he keeps very much to himself and it is his unwillingness to be completely open that can cause relationships to flounder. Others, particularly those who manage to break through the Monkey façade, may become suspicious of his sometimes evasive nature. The Monkey does like to be loved, but giving love to another is, for him, a major step and not one he finds easy.

However, once the Monkey has made a commitment, then he can be a loyal, generous and most attentive partner. He is all for making his home life full and varied. He does, after all, possess a delicious sense of fun and likes to keep himself – and others in his household – involved in so much. Should he become a parent, he will really delight in the upbringing of his children, sharing in their games and jokes, encouraging their imagination and thoroughly enjoying himself, almost reliving the wonder of his own childhood years.

The male Monkey has an agreeable and outgoing nature and is able to get on well with others. However, for all his *bonhomie*, he can be secretive, evasive and at times artful. His personality and quick wits do, though, usually enable him to get his way and he can be most persuasive. He is also prepared to take risks to achieve what he wants, considering that if things do not go his way his resourcefulness will come to his rescue, and on some occasions it will! In appearance the male Monkey is smart and often dresses with style. He is, after all, always keen to make a favourable impression.

The female Monkey also takes a great deal of care with her appearance, choosing her clothes well. She has a good eye for detail, style and colour. She also plays especial attention to her hair and likes to experiment with different looks. In nature, she is vivacious, a keen socializer and will have a great many friends. She is also confident in manner and this, together with her wide interests, enables her to enjoy a good rapport with many. She is observant and perceptive and once she has set her mind on what she wants, she often gets her way. The female Monkey has style, panache and ambition.

Keen, active and resourceful, the Monkey makes much of life. Sometimes he may even treat it as a game, manoeuvring himself into good positions, sorting out problems and using his wits to secure his ends. Throughout his life, he will achieve a great deal. Monkeys born in the summer are considered the luckiest, but with their alert and perceptive natures, all are indeed capable of leading rich, interesting and often colourful lives.

SUCCESS AND WORK

As with so much of his life, the Monkey sets about his work with much gusto. Always keen to make the most of himself, his ideas and situation, he is both enterprising and ambitious. He is also confident that he possesses the ways and means to secure his objectives. Sometimes these ways may not always be ethical – the Monkey is a great one for taking short cuts or bending the rules – but he certainly possesses the talents and drive to go far.

In addition he is observant and blessed with an exceedingly good memory and he uses this to often impressive effect. For instance, when speaking with a colleague, he may enquire about a family member his colleague mentioned once. The Monkey has a great personal touch.

The Monkey is also adept at spotting opportunities or loop-holes that he could use to his advantage. Indeed, he is all for profiting from situations. In addition, he is a good problem-solver and many a time he will come up with a solution to a problem that had thwarted others. Again, he will use this talent to excellent effect.

There are, though, several factors that can undermine the Monkey's success and he would do well to watch these. In particular, he likes to involve himself in a great deal and, as a consequence, can sometimes become distracted or spread his energies too widely. Also, the crafty ways that the Monkey can resort to, while often successful, can diminish him in the eyes of others. He may be well liked, but in many positions trust is essential.

Being so versatile, Monkeys can be tempted into a wide range of careers. However, the Monkey does particularly like positions which offer a challenge and allow him to make good use of his ideas and skills. He is certainly not one for sticking to set and sometimes monotonous routines. Monkeys can excel in careers which allow for creativity, and whether in the media, PR, marketing or the arts (particularly in writing, the theatre or music), the Monkey's originality and talents can be much in demand.

With his genial and persuasive manner, the Monkey can also make an effective retailer and, with his head for figures, do well in the financial sector. His fine linguistic abilities can also open up many other careers for him and, in almost any capacity, he can make an impression.

The Monkey is adaptable and versatile and is certainly keen on action. With persistence and application, he has the talent to go far in his chosen line of work.

SUCCESS AND MONEY

With his keen wits, head for figures and ability to profit from opportunities, the Monkey certainly has money-making skills. He is resourceful and enterprising and is capable of earning a good income.

The Monkey enjoys money. It enables him to have a good time and live in style. Whether going out with family or friends, to whom he can be most generous, or buying himself some treat, the Monkey likes to have money at his disposal. In fact he does sometimes spend too freely. Money will flow both in and out of his accounts on a fairly regular basis.

The Monkey is a thoughtful provider and is always willing to look after family members, even sometimes spoiling them. He can, though, be less generous to those outside his immediate circle and is not renowned for his charity.

Although the Monkey's judgement in financial matters is usually good, there will be times when the possible rewards of a certain action may blind him to the true risks involved. Sometimes he could take one risk too many and lose out. Similarly, his keenness to profit from situations can tempt him into using devious means and again there is a chance that one day these could backfire. The Monkey does like to push his luck and while often successful, he does still run the risk of losing a lot in a moment of rashness.

However, while the Monkey will make some mistakes, he is a quick learner and can recover well from any setback. His talents and resourcefulness will invariably see him through.

In general, the Monkey can enjoy a good level of success in money matters. However, he does need to try to build up his assets and plan for the longer term. Although he likes to spend, he should still keep some funds in reserve. He also needs to be careful with any risks or speculation, taking the time to consider all the implications. He may be shrewd, but greed or a winning streak could lead him into false complacency and he must remain aware of this. In money matters, more control and caution would not go amiss.

SUCCESS IN LOVE

Friendly and well informed with a good sense of humour, the Monkey makes popular company. And he so desires someone to love and share his life with.

In his adolescence the Monkey is certainly flirtatious and will enjoy many casual romances. However, the path of love is not an easy one for him. Although he likes being with others, he keeps his true feelings very much to himself. He may appear genial and open and someone you can confide in, but he himself will rarely confide in others. The Monkey relies so much upon himself that in some ways he considers himself self-contained. Making a commitment to another is a big step for him and when relationships appear to be turning more serious, some Monkeys start to become wary. They start questioning the relationship, their partner and their own feelings, wondering whether any love they feel is actually 'the real thing'. While so keen to have a partner, the Monkey can be too analytical and this can cause much heartache and in some cases disappointment. Love is a treasure to be enjoyed and nurtured. It does not always need or bear up to examination – and the Monkey should try to resist doing this and let his heart rule instead. He will find the path of love so much happier as a result.

In seeking a partner the Monkey will find the greatest happiness with someone who is easy-going and tolerant, has wide interests and is willing to accept – and enjoy – the Monkey's rich and multi-faceted personality. Life with a Monkey can be enjoyable and different. And in return, the Monkey will be a loyal, considerate and generous partner.

SUCCESS WITH OTHERS

The Monkey has a great way with others. Friendly, amusing and interesting, he makes popular company. While he can get on so well with so many – and the Monkey *does* like making a favourable impression – he will find there are some signs he is more at ease with than others.

With a Rat

The Monkey has a great liking for the resourceful Rat and relations between the two signs are often good.

In the parent–child relationship, there will be a particularly close bond between Monkey parent and Rat child. Both are keen and imaginative and they will have many interests they can share and enjoy. The young Rat will do much to live up to his Monkey parent's expectations.

As colleagues, these two are supremely resourceful and adept at seeking out and making the most of opportunities. They have ideas, talent and ambition. The Monkey will find the Rat an inspirational colleague and by combining their talents, they can make a successful team. However, to maximize their potential they do need to work closely together and should either be tempted to outsmart the other, then so much could be lost.

In love, they are ideally suited. With similar tastes and many interests they can share, these two will live life to the full. The Monkey will especially value the Rat's loyal and supportive ways as well as his fine abilities as a homemaker. They make an excellent match.

With an Ox

The Monkey has a great admiration for the solid and reliable ways of the Ox and, although they are so different in personality, relations between them can be good.

In the parent–child relationship, the Monkey parent can be a positive influence on the Ox child, helping to make the young Ox more outgoing as well as encouraging him to take up a broader range of interests. Theirs can be a sound relationship.

As colleagues, their different skills and strengths complement each other and together they can make a successful team. The Monkey will particularly gain from the Ox's more practical and persistent approach as well as respect his judgement. They make a good combination.

In love, their different personalities blend well and both will gain much from their relationship. The Monkey will especially appreciate the loyal and dependable nature of an Ox partner as well as finding him a steadying influence. These two will love and care for each other.

With the Tiger

The Monkey finds the Tiger lively and enjoyable company, although when they get to know each other better, problems could start to surface.

In the parent–child relationship, the Monkey parent will admire the enterprising and resourceful spirit of the young Tiger and, while there will be the inevitable clash when the young Tiger shows his independent and self-willed side, there will be a good bond between them.

As colleagues, these two have ideas aplenty and both are highly enterprising. However, personality differences could undermine their work, with the Monkey resisting the Tiger's desire to dominate. Each will prefer to stick to his own ways rather than collaborate.

In love, their lively, sociable and fun-loving natures could bring them together, but problems will lurk. The Monkey, who so likes to be involved in everything, will find it hard to accept the Tiger's somewhat independent streak and, with each being strong-willed and wanting to prevail, there will need to be a great deal of compromise if their relationship is to endure.

With a Rabbit

The Monkey enjoys a good rapport with the quiet and amiable Rabbit and, with interests in common, the two signs get on well.

In the parent–child relationship, the Monkey parent will be proud of his good-natured and able Rabbit child and will guide him well, encouraging the young Rabbit to become more outwardly confident. There will be an affectionate bond between them.

As colleagues, relations between the Monkey and Rabbit could be at their most awkward. The Monkey is all for action, for taking risks and for getting speedy results, while the Rabbit likes to proceed carefully. The Monkey will view the Rabbit as a restraining influence and as a result there will be a general lack of accord between them.

In love, the Monkey and Rabbit are well suited. Although their personalities are very different, they do complement each other and both will gain much from their relationship. In addition to their liking for the finer things in life, socializing and enjoying conversation, they have a great many other interests which they can share. The Monkey will regard the Rabbit as a wise, loving and caring partner and they make a good and often enduring match.

With a Dragon

The Monkey admires the lively and spirited ways of the Dragon and the two signs get on well together.

In the parent–child relationship, the Monkey parent will particularly admire the resourceful and enterprising nature of the Dragon child and will do much to support and encourage him. There will be much love between them.

As colleagues, the Monkey and Dragon are ambitious and work well together. The Monkey admires the Dragon's enterprise and zest, and by combining their fine business skills, they can enjoy a good level of success.

In love, the Monkey and Dragon understand each other well and can form a close and meaningful relationship. They both like to lead active lifestyles and will have a multitude of different interests to enjoy. Both are keen socializers and the Monkey will appreciate the Dragon's lively, confident and supportive manner. They can find much happiness together.

With the Snake

The Monkey is often intrigued by the quiet and thoughtful Snake, but how well they get on does depend on the situation.

In the parent–child relationship, the Monkey parent may not find the quiet and reserved Snake child the easiest to understand or handle. The Monkey parent will encourage him, but the young Snake may not always be receptive. It will take much patience and understanding before a satisfactory rapport can be established.

As colleagues, differences of opinion could well arise. The Monkey is keen on action and getting things done and will soon become impatient with the Snake's more cautious and calculating attitude. As both can be evasive and keep their thoughts to themselves, it will not be too long before they go their separate ways.

In love, the Monkey and Snake often fascinate each other and, once attracted, can form a close and very special relationship. The Monkey will find the Snake a thoughtful and considerate partner and will appreciate his often rich humour and gentle ways. The pair understand and support each other, with their different strengths often being complementary. They can make a good and lasting match.

With a Horse

The Monkey is well aware of the Horse's strong-willed and independent nature and, as a result, will be wary of him. Relations between the two signs are often cool and reserved.

In the parent–child relationship, the Monkey parent, while so admiring the Horse child's keen and diligent nature, could find the young Horse's independent and self-willed ways difficult to deal with. Theirs will be a tricky relationship.

As colleagues, if they are able to put their personal feelings to one side and combine their considerable strengths, then the Horse and Monkey could achieve a great deal. Both are hardworking, ambitious and enterprising. However, each will want to prevail and their mutual wariness could prevent them from ever realizing their combined potential.

In love, their lively and sociable natures may bring them together, but the way ahead will be tricky. Both will want to dominate the relationship and, due to their proud and strong-willed natures, compromise is not something that comes easily to either. Also, while the Monkey may admire the Horse's lively and enterprising ways, he will find his quick temper and impatient attitude difficult to bear. As a result, it will take an exceptional Monkey–Horse couple to make their relationship work.

With a Goat

The Monkey likes the easy-going and companionable Goat and relations between the two signs are good.

In the parent–child relationship, there is a close and loving rapport between Monkey parent and Goat child. The young Goat will respond well to the enthusiasm of a lively Monkey parent and will strive to please. Also, the Monkey's attentive and often positive temperament can be a wonderful antidote to the young Goat's anxious tendencies.

As colleagues, the Monkey will be quick to recognize the talents of the creative and imaginative Goat and will do much to encourage him. These two like each other and work well together. By combining their different talents and skills, they can achieve considerable success.

In love, the Monkey and Goat are good for each other. Both enjoy the finer things in life and there will be much laughter, happiness and variety to their relationship. They also appreciate each other's strengths, with the Monkey admiring the Goat's talents as a homemaker as well as valuing his affectionate nature. They are well suited and can make a close and loving couple.

With another Monkey

With his wide interests, great sense of fun and sociable nature, the Monkey gets on well with another Monkey and relations between them can be excellent.

In the parent–child relationship, the Monkey parent will enjoy a great rapport with his Monkey child. The parent will do much to encourage and satisfy the child's enquiring mind as well as joining in with so many of his interests and games. There will be much love, respect and fun to their relationship.

As colleagues, two Monkeys have ideas, ambition and tremendous guile. However, to succeed they will need to remain focused and work towards specific objectives. If not, these two could head in so many different directions that the success they are so capable of achieving could be elusive. Also, with the Monkey's competitive streak, each must resist the temptation to outwit the other. Again, discipline and firmness of purpose will be so essential to their success.

In love, two Monkeys can enjoy a happy and harmonious relationship. With their many interests and talents for enjoying themselves, there will be activity, fun and variety to their relationship – and also much laughter. Each will encourage and support the other and together they can make a splendid match.

With a Rooster

The Monkey admires many of the Rooster's qualities, but their personalities do not always gel.

In the parent–child relationship, the conscientious Rooster child will respond well to the Monkey parent's enthusiastic and supportive nature and try to live up to his parent's expectations. They will respect each other.

As colleagues, the Monkey and Rooster have very different approaches to work. The Monkey likes action and relies heavily on his wits and resourcefulness, while the Rooster is a meticulous planner and organizer. The Monkey will soon lose patience with the Rooster's methods and, with little accord between them, they will quickly go their separate ways.

In love, the Monkey and Rooster may both be outgoing types and keen socializers, but there are many differences that will need to be reconciled if their relationship is to endure. In particular the Monkey could find it hard to accept the Rooster's more ordered lifestyle as well as lose patience with his blunt and candid nature. The Monkey is all for a more easy-going and varied life. The way ahead will be difficult.

⚞ With a Dog

Despite their many personality differences, the Monkey has a high regard for the sincere and dutiful Dog and relations between them will often be good as well as mutually beneficial.

In the parent–child relationship, the Monkey parent will do much to encourage the Dog child and to build up his confidence and self-esteem. They will be a good bond between them.

As colleagues, by combining their different strengths, the Monkey and Dog can make an effective combination. The Monkey will benefit from the Dog's more disciplined and persistent approach and as both are keen to make the most of themselves, they can do well together.

In love, this can be a beneficial relationship and one which will often grow stronger as each gets to know and appreciate the other. The Monkey will value the Dog's affectionate and supportive ways and regard him as a trusted and loyal ally. The pair complement each other and can find much happiness.

⚞ With a Pig

The Monkey has a great fondness for the genial and fun-loving Pig and relations between the two signs are often excellent.

In the parent–child relationship, the Pig child responds well to the lively, enthusiastic and attentive ways of the Monkey parent and there will be a close and loving bond between them.

As colleagues, each has a high regard for the other and by combining their skills and talents, they can enjoy a good level of success. The Monkey has a great admiration for the Pig's tenacity and commercial acumen and the Pig can be a helpful influence for the Monkey, especially in channelling his energy in a purposeful way.

In love, the Monkey and Pig can make a close and loving match. With their lively natures, many interests, fondness for the good life and genial dispositions, they enjoy a great understanding. The Monkey will value having such an easy-going, amiable and supportive partner. Both will gain a lot from their relationship and together they can find much happiness.

SUCCESS THROUGH LIFE

As the Monkey is interested in so much and keeps himself so active, his life is invariably full and varied. Certain stages will be easier and more successful than others, but the Monkey will always endeavour to make the most of his situation and use his talents to good effect. He has a great and infectious spirit and this will serve him well throughout his life.

In his childhood years, the Monkey's inquisitive nature will quickly become evident. Forever asking questions, the young Monkey will delight in finding out about everything. Admittedly he may sometimes be exasperating and his inquisitive nature can lead him into difficult situations, but he will learn quickly. At school he will often impress, especially with his ability to take in and remember so much. But while he may be a good scholar, his mischievous and jokey nature may not always be so appreciated!

The Monkey's early adult years can be a trickier time. While so popular with his peers, his early romances may cause him anguish as he grapples with the complexities of love and with his own feelings, which he finds so hard to explain. Entering into a commitment with another is a particularly major (and sometimes daunting) step for the Monkey to take.

In the Monkey's work, too, the first years will often teach him some hard lessons. While so keen to progress, he could find some of his ideas or the short cuts he likes to take do not always work out. And although he is eager and ambitious, sometimes his lack of experience will prevent him from making the swift progress he would like. Advancing up the ladder of success can take time – sometimes longer than the Monkey has envisaged. In general, his early adult years will be challenging and sometimes difficult, but he will learn a great deal from them.

As middle age approaches the Monkey will be more in command of his situation and feel much more fulfilled. Often his efforts will have allowed him to become established in a particular line of work and, resourceful as ever, he will make the most of his expertise and skills. Many Monkeys will also delight in their family and their lively social life as well as their many different interests.

As time goes on, the Monkey could, though, have some difficulty in adapting to old age. A gentler lifestyle does not come easily to him and he could miss some of the activity and companionship that has characterized so much of his life. However, he will enjoy following the progress of family members as well as maintaining his many interests and his social life. The Monkey is all for using his time well. For him, life is a treasure to be lived and enjoyed. And he often succeeds admirably.

FAMOUS MONKEYS

Gillian Anderson, Jennifer Aniston, Francesca Annis, Christina Aquilera, Michael Aspel, J. M. Barrie, Julius Caesar, Johnny Cash, Jacques Chirac, Joe Cocker, Colette, David Copperfield, Patricia Cornwell, Joan Crawford, Leonardo da Vinci, Timothy Dalton, Bette Davis, Danny De Vito, Celine Dion, Michael

Douglas, Mia Farrow, F. Scott Fitzgerald, Ian Fleming, Dick Francis, Paul Gauguin, Jerry Hall, Tom Hanks, Martina Hingis, Harry Houdini, Lyndon B. Johnson, Buster Keaton, Gladys Knight, Bob Marley, Walter Matthau, Kylie Minogue, Peter O'Toole, Anthony Perkins, Debbie Reynolds, Little Richard, Mickey Rooney, Eleanor Roosevelt, Diana Ross, Bertrand Russell, Gerhard Schröder, Michael Schumacher, Tom Selleck, Omar Sharif, Samuel Smiles, Wilbur Smith, Will Smith, Rod Stewart, Jacques Tati, Elizabeth Taylor, Dame Kiri Te Kanawa, Harry Truman, Venus Williams.

SUCCESS TIPS FOR THE MONKEY

The Monkey has a sense of spontaneity about him. He is all for action and swift results. If results are a long time in coming, then he could well lose interest and turn his attention to something else. However, in order to progress, it *is* necessary to persevere and to allow time to build up experience and skills, and the Monkey must accept this. He has the ability to achieve a great deal, but he needs to be more dedicated and constant in the pursuit of what he wants, as well as allow himself the time to achieve his goals.

The Monkey has great confidence in himself and his abilities and as a result he tends not to seek or indeed listen to the advice of others. This not only prevents him from benefiting from advice but can also deny him support and make him appear arrogant. The Monkey may have charm and a friendly nature, but if he is not careful, he could undermine this by his exclusivity and his sometimes superior manner. He does have wonderful personal skills and should use them to his advantage. If he is prepared to listen to others, he will not only learn in the process, but will also often be better able to win support. To be more successful, the Monkey does need to pay more heed to others.

The Monkey lives very much in the present, but does not always adequately plan for the future. In his work he would do well to give more consideration to the skills, qualifications and experience he needs in order to progress. By planning ahead more, he will often find it much easier to advance.

Being so versatile and inquisitive, the Monkey does have wide interests but sometimes these can lead him to dabble rather than become truly involved in certain activities. He can be a Jack of all trades and master of none. While the Monkey may like dabbling, he will often find that he will get greater satisfaction by actually mastering specific activities. By becoming more proficient he can find an interest taking on greater meaning and possibly opening up new doors for him. Also the discipline required to master specific interests and skills can assist the Monkey in other spheres of his life and will help him to become more focused.

The Monkey possesses some very original talents. He is inventive, innovative, resourceful and a wonderful problem-solver. By promoting himself and furthering his ideas, he can make a considerable impression. But to be successful, he does need to persist more and win support for what he does. He may like to be his own man, but success is also dependent on the reaction and support of others.

SOME FINAL THOUGHTS FROM MONKEYS

Man needs, for his happiness, not only the enjoyment of this or that, but hope and enterprise and change.
Bertrand Russell

Anything you're good at contributes to happiness.
Bertrand Russell

'Where there is a will there is a way' is an old and true saying.
He who resolves upon doing a thing, by that very resolution
often scales the barriers to it, and secures its achievement.
Samuel Smiles

Those who are the most persistent, and work in the true spirit,
will invariably be the most successful.
Samuel Smiles

The battle of life is, in most cases, fought uphill; and to win it
without a struggle were perhaps to win it without honour. If
there were no difficulties, there would be no success; if there
were nothing to struggle for, there would be nothing to be
achieved.
Samuel Smiles

Great results cannot be achieved at once, and we must be satis-
fied to advance in life as we walk – step by step.
Samuel Smiles

Self respect is the noblest garment with which a man may clothe
himself – the most elevating feeling with which the mind can be
inspired.
Samuel Smiles

Life will always be to a large extent what we ourselves make it.
Samuel Smiles

Life was meant to be lived, and curiosity must be kept alive. One must never, for whatever reason, turn one's back on life.
Eleanor Roosevelt

The future belongs to those who believe in the beauty of their dreams.
Eleanor Roosevelt

The
Rooster

Greeting every morning with a loud crowing, the Rooster seems to have assumed the responsibility of chief time-keeper by heralding the start of another day. Having woken everyone up, he will strut around the farmyard, his beady eyes taking in every detail, including the tiniest of morsels to peck at. Little gets past him. Orderly, efficient and methodical, the Rooster makes his presence felt. And so do many born under the tenth Chinese sign.

Above all, the Rooster is well-meaning and he takes his responsibilities seriously. Whether it is in his home or work, he likes to plan, oversee and make sure all is in order. To secure this the Rooster does need to assert his authority and, being born under the sign of candour, will not hesitate to speak his mind, regardless of what others may think. While he may some-times offend, he is nevertheless respected for his frank and sincere approach. In addition, the Rooster is honourable in his dealings and as a result inspires both confidence and trust.

The Rooster also possesses a sharp mind. Often widely read, he keeps himself well informed and, being highly observant, remembers all sorts of details. He is an effective communicator and particularly revels in debate. His attention to fine detail, his eloquence and style make him a compelling and persuasive speaker. He has a ready wit and can be a fine raconteur.

In his manner, the Rooster is outgoing and friendly. He enjoys socializing and his sincerity and interest in others make people warm to him. He is confident and self-assured and while he may sometimes lack tact, at least there is no hedging with the Rooster. You know where he stands and he is always upfront.

The Rooster certainly has qualities that make for an interesting and often successful life. But he also has his failings which, unless watched, can jeopardize the success he could otherwise enjoy.

In particular the Rooster can be pernickety. With his desire to getting everything right, he can fuss over the smallest of details and his nit-picking and fastidiousness can sometimes grate. In addition, the Rooster's attention to detail can lead him to overlook some of the broader implications of what he is tackling. It is admirable to set high standards, but to continually strive for perfection can be costly, particularly in terms of time.

Also, the Rooster can sometimes come across as vain. With his dominant personality, he enjoys being the centre of attention and this can lead him to exaggerate his manner and achievements. To some, he can appear arrogant and boastful and this can tell against him and sometimes deny him valuable support. This is something the Rooster should watch. Some of his personality is for show – he *does* like to be noticed – but, taken too far, this can be counter-productive.

In fact, although on the outside, the Rooster may seem self-assured, on the inside it can be a different picture. He may appear bold and confident, but this sometimes masks a more insecure and vulnerable side. The Rooster may not show it, but he can worry a great deal. This does not fit in with his image and he will rarely reveal his feelings, but he may nevertheless be anxious about what others might think of him and whether his actions are the right ones. At particularly worrying or stressful times, rather than keep his feelings to himself, it really would be in the Rooster's interests to seek advice, reassurance and support. He himself does so much to help others that he should at least give them the chance to reciprocate, especially when he feels under pressure.

Whatever his inner insecurities, the Rooster is well intentioned and always eager to give his best. In his work he is reliable and conscientious. He is also a great planner – many a Rooster will have mapped out the whole course of his life at an early age. Admittedly such plans change and some will never materialize, but the Rooster will always have a goal to strive for and can enjoy a good level of success in his career.

He also has considerable earning ability, although there are quite a few Roosters who tend to spend freely as well. Not only does the Rooster have expensive tastes, but he also spends a lot while out socializing. However, he is aware of his commitments and while there are some Roosters who may find it hard to save, usually the Rooster manages his money well.

The time of day the Rooster is born can make quite a difference to his personality. Those born between the hours of sunrise and sunset, 5–7 a.m. and 5–7 p.m., are more extrovert, while those born at night tend to be quieter and more reserved. All Roosters, though, possess a distinctive charm and presence that commands attention. And in matters of the heart the Rooster will have no shortage of admirers.

Both male and female Roosters conduct themselves well and in style. The male is smart in appearance and often makes a dashing figure. He sets about so much of what he does in an orderly and precise way and is frank in his views. However, while he does have a more serious side and is determined and ambitious, he has considerable charm, a good sense of humour and a caring nature. He is also highly perceptive, with his advice and opinions being well regarded.

The female Rooster knows how to impress. In appearance she aims for practical but good-quality clothes and has a fine appreciation of style and co-ordination. She is invariably well-groomed. She is also highly organized and sets about her various activities with much care. Whether it is running her home, organizing family activities or doing her work, she is invariably in command of the situation and knows what she wants to achieve. However, while she takes her responsibilities seriously, she does possess a good sense of fun. A keen socializer, she will have a great many friends. Indeed, others will marvel at just how much she is able to accomplish and how well she organizes the various aspects of her life.

If the Rooster becomes a parent he will be caring and attentive but also strict and will set his children high standards. As a result, they will learn much from him and certainly be well equipped (and organized enough) to cope when they are old enough to leave home.

All Roosters take great pride in their home and will keep it neat, orderly and clean. The Rooster also derives much satisfaction from housework and in getting his home as he wants – and woe betide any member of the household who is particularly untidy or spoils the Rooster's work! In the home, the Rooster reigns supreme and he does have high expectations. He also likes his comforts and as well as equipping his home with many appliances to make life easier, he could have a penchant for interesting but practical gadgets.

In addition to the care the Rooster gives to his home, he is often a keen gardener. Many Roosters will take pleasure in planning their garden and tending their plants as well as being a dab hand with the pruner! The Rooster's love of the outdoors also draws him to pursuits such as walking, angling or following sport. He has a liking for the arts and, in addition to being a keen reader, could also enjoy writing or involving himself in the performing arts, including amateur dramatics or singing. As he likes company and shines in group activities, he can also be an active member of a club or special-interest society.

Roosters born in the spring are considered the luckiest and while all will have to strive hard for the success they will enjoy, the Rooster is destined to lead an interesting and fulfilling life. Being so active and caring, he will also make a difference in the lives of many as well as hold a truly special place in the hearts of his loved ones.

SUCCESS AND WORK

The Rooster has great potential. Not only is he efficient in the conduct of his duties, but he is also prepared to put himself forward and to take action to secure what he wants. He has drive, ambition and ability. He is perceptive, has a good memory and a quick grasp of detail. He also possesses a forceful personality. He certainly has no hesitation in expressing his views and is a most effective communicator. His style can help him get noticed – the Rooster tends to stand out. He is very adept at his own PR!

The Rooster certainly has the abilities to achieve a good level of success in his work. However, there are certain points he does need to watch. In particular, he can be outspoken and his lack of tact can sometimes make others wary of him and lose him support. He can fuss over petty and minor details, sometimes even becoming obsessed with them, and this tendency can, if he is not careful, take his attention away from his main objectives and waste much of his time.

In choosing his career, the Rooster will enjoy positions which offer a challenge and allow him to use his abilities to organize and manage to good effect. As a result, some Roosters will be drawn to administrative roles, the financial sector or running their own business. The Rooster does, after all, like to be at the helm!

With his buoyant personality, he also could be attracted to the performing arts, while his ability to put his ideas across so well can make him an effective writer, teacher or politician. In addition, with their presentation skills, Roosters can enjoy considerable success in marketing, commerce and PR. The Rooster will also take great pride if his position requires a uniform and whether in the military, the police or some other profession, he will invariably look distinguished as well as perform his duties with much pride.

The Rooster works hard and he possesses both the drive and the energy to make an impact in whichever career he does choose to enter.

SUCCESS AND MONEY

With his methodical nature and eye for detail, the Rooster is well equipped to deal with money. He likes order and will often keep meticulous records. He also possesses good financial judgement and when he has funds, he can be a shrewd investor.

However, there are some Roosters who still run into problems. Some like to live on a grand scale and spend freely, particularly when out socializing or wanting to impress. The generosity and self-indulgence of these Roosters will prevent them from saving much or from making provision for the future. Although they will be aware of their commitments and the amount they spend, it would certainly be in their interests to exercise a greater control over their purse strings and give more thought to the longer term.

However, just as there are extrovert Roosters and much quieter Roosters, so there are Roosters who are the complete opposite of the spendthrift sort and who save as much as they can, keenly watching interest rates and always eager to maximize their returns. With such control and fine judgement, these Roosters can certainly become materially well off.

As with so much of the Rooster character, it is a case of striking a fine balance. The Rooster certainly has the ability to enjoy a good level of success in money matters, especially with his capacity to earn, select investments and keep financial records, but he should seek a balance between spending and saving. If he can do this – and many Roosters do in the end manage it – then he can be assured of living in fine style as well as having some assets in reserve, with these usually being sensibly invested.

SUCCESS IN LOVE

Sociable, outgoing and presentable, the Rooster will have no shortage of admirers. His fine qualities and generous nature will lead to many glorious and exciting romances, and the Rooster is certainly passionate and loving. But while love can bring such wondrous delights, it can also bring anxiety and heartbreak.

In love, the Rooster has just so much to offer, but his own attitude may not always help. He does speak his mind and his strong opinions and forthright nature may turn some against him. True he may not want to hurt others, but for the more sensitive, his matter-of-fact tones will cause distress. Also, while the Rooster may be forthcoming about so much, he does not always find it so easy to reveal his innermost feelings. This can make him appear aloof when a few tender words from his heart could make all the difference. He can also suffer from jealousy and cause himself much emotional anguish by dwelling over certain aspects of a relationship. He does so like everything to be right.

Underneath his forceful and blustering exterior, however, the Rooster possesses a loving, warm and kindly heart. He does so want to be loved. And in his youth and early adult years he will often experience the ecstasy (and pain) which love can bring.

As with so much in life, in love the Rooster does proceed with care and rather than rush into an unsatisfactory commitment, he is prepared to wait for Mr or Ms Right. Ideally, this person will need to accept that the Rooster does have a dominant nature and may sometimes be candid as well as pernickety, but in return the Rooster will strive to make sure that his home is well run and that all are well provided for, and he will take his responsibilities as a partner – and parent – very seriously. He is honest and dependable and underneath his blustering and colourful exterior, he does possess a kind and well-meaning nature.

Life with the Rooster may not always be easy, but for the right partner it can be rich and so wonderfully rewarding.

SUCCESS WITH OTHERS

The Rooster is a keen socializer and takes pleasure in getting to know others. With his vibrant and outgoing personality he will be sure to impress. However, while he can enjoy good relations with many, there are some signs he will form a better understanding with than others.

With a Rat

The Rooster may, for a time, find the Rat interesting company, particularly as both like conversation, but sooner rather than later their candid natures will get the better of them and relations will deteriorate.

In the parent–child relationship, the adventurous Rat child could find life in a regimented Rooster household a little stifling and there will be a certain edginess to their relationship. However, despite the occasional clash, the Rooster parent will be a good influence, providing discipline and encouragement as well as instilling the virtues of order and planning, something which it will be useful for the young Rat to learn.

As colleagues, differences in style and approach will make relations difficult. The methodical and careful Rooster will view the Rat's resourceful and quick-witted ways with disfavour and there will be little trust or accord between them. Not a successful combination.

In love, their mutual interests can draw them together, particularly as both are so outgoing and sociable. But once the initial attraction wanes, relations could become difficult. Both are strong-minded and candid, and the Rooster, who is so orderly, will soon tire of the Rat's more carefree ways. With the Rat being thrifty and the Rooster more of a spendthrift, their different attitudes to money could also cause problems. These two will have many hurdles to overcome if their relationship is to endure.

With an Ox

The Rooster admires the solid and dependable nature of the Ox and relations between these two signs are good.

In the parent–child relationship, the Ox child will thrive in a well-ordered Rooster household. The Rooster parent will be effective at drawing out the best qualities of a young Ox, encouraging him to be more outgoing as well as giving him the time and opportunity to develop in his own way. There will be a close and loving bond between them.

As colleagues, these two are efficient, methodical and take great pride in what they do. They like and respect each other, with the Rooster appreciating the Ox's strong will and dedicated approach. Together they have the drive and abilities to achieve great success.

In love, the Rooster and Ox are often drawn to each other and can find much happiness. They have similar outlooks and there will be a good understanding between them. They also share many interests. Both are practical and methodical and are often fond of gardening, the countryside and outdoor pursuits. The Rooster will draw particular strength from the Ox's dependable and redoubtable nature. These two signs complement each other and a match between them will often be successful and rewarding.

With a Tiger

With his energy, wide interests and outgoing ways, the Rooster will find the Tiger engaging company. However, these two are forthright and self-willed and differences of opinion could often arise.

In the parent–child relationship, the Rooster parent will admire the enterprise and wide interests of his earnest Tiger child, although sometimes the young Tiger's high spirits and independent ways will lead to clashes, especially as the Rooster parent is so strong on discipline.

As colleagues, they could gain much from each other, with the Rooster benefiting from the Tiger's innovative and enterprising ways. But each will want to take the lead and, as both can be so forthright, disagreements could quickly undermine what could have been a successful relationship. If they can be more tolerant of each other and pool their different strengths, however, then these two could go far.

In love, the Rooster and Tiger will often fascinate each other. They are both outgoing and are keen socializers, with the Rooster particularly admiring the Tiger's confident and earnest nature. But each will want to prevail and as they are both forthright in expressing their views, relations could often become heated and volatile. Also, the methodical Rooster could find the Tiger's restless and impulsive nature a trial. A challenging match.

⤛ With a Rabbit

Although there are many qualities in the Rabbit that the Rooster admires, their personalities do not gel and relations between them will often be difficult.

In the parent–child relationship, the Rooster parent will teach the Rabbit child well, but the parent's matter-of-fact manner and sharp tongue could trouble the more sensitive Rabbit. Relations between them will need careful handling.

As colleagues, there will be a lack of accord. The Rooster is active and outgoing in style while the Rabbit is quiet, reserved and cautious. While some signs can combine their different qualities to good effect, the general antipathy between Rooster and Rabbit will prevent this. Not a successful combination.

In love, the Rooster may be attracted by the Rabbit's affectionate, kindly and refined ways, but there is a wide gulf between them. The Rooster likes a busy lifestyle while the Rabbit prefers a more sedate and peaceful existence. They live their lives at different speeds and it will take an exceptional couple to make the adjustments necessary for their relationship to work. A difficult match.

ᐤ With a Dragon

The Rooster is very much attracted by the style, enthusiasm and colourful personality of the Dragon and relations between the two signs are mostly good.

In the parent–child relationship, relations will be at their most awkward. The Rooster parent is strict and expects to be obeyed, but the young Dragon possesses a determined streak and there will be times when their strong wills will clash. However, while relations will sometimes call for careful handling, the Dragon child will learn a great deal from his efficient and caring Rooster parent.

As colleagues, the Dragon and Rooster work well together and by combining their individual strengths, they can achieve considerable success. The Rooster will be inspired by the Dragon's enterprising and determined nature.

In love, the Rooster and Dragon can find much happiness. Both are outgoing and they will have many interests in common. They also understand each other well, with both being aware that there is another level beneath their redoubtable façades, a level that desires tender love, support and reassurance. The Rooster will find the Dragon is supportive as well as sincere and often so lively. They are well matched.

ᐤ With a Snake

The Rooster has a great admiration for the quiet and thoughtful Snake and the two signs can build up an excellent rapport.

In the parent–child relationship, the Rooster parent will do much to encourage and support the Snake child, helping him to become more confident, and the young Snake will benefit from the Rooster's guidance. There will be much love between them.

As colleagues, the Rooster and Snake complement each other

well, with the Rooster appreciating the Snake's careful but often canny approach. Although their styles may be different, they are both ambitious, each will respect the other and together they can enjoy considerable success.

In love, the Rooster and Snake are good for each other, with the Rooster appreciating the Snake's calm temperament as well as kindly and supportive nature. They also have much in common, with both possessing cultured tastes and enjoying conversation. Together the Snake and Rooster can find much happiness.

⚞ With a Horse

Lively and sociable, the Horse and Rooster can for a time get on well, but their strong-willed and forthright natures will, in the end, cause differences between them.

In the parent–child relationship, relations between Rooster parent and Horse child will be tricky. The Rooster parent so wants to support, guide and love the Horse child, but the Horse child can be self-willed and independent-minded and may not always be as responsive as the Rooster parent would like.

As colleagues, the Rooster and Horse are both ambitious and by combining their strengths, they can achieve much. The Rooster will draw strength from the Horse's industrious and dedicated approach and each will do much to motivate the other.

In love, the Rooster and Horse can often be attracted to each other. They are both keen socializers and enjoy active lifestyles. However, while there can be much fun and activity to their relationship, particularly in the early days, problems could lurk. In particular, as both have dominant personalities, each will want to prevail and their forthright natures could lead to some heated exchanges. The Rooster, who so likes organization, could find it difficult to accept the Horse's more restless tendencies. It will take much care and many adjustments on both sides if their relationship is to endure.

With a Goat

The Rooster will soon become exasperated by the whimsical and easy-going Goat and relations between them will be poor.

In the parent–child relationship, the sensitive Goat child could find the orderly and forthright nature of the Rooster parent hard to bear. The Goat child will strive to please and the Rooster parent will try to be considerate, but there will be an uneasiness to their relationship.

As colleagues, their different approaches will cause many problems and they will find it difficult to work satisfactorily with each other. The highly organized and disciplined Rooster will not be tolerant of the Goat's more easy-going and imaginative approach. The Rooster is all for practicalities and discipline.

In love, this will be a challenging match. The Rooster likes a structured and ordered lifestyle, while the Goat prefers a much more relaxed and laid-back existence. The Rooster will lack the patience to cope with the Goat's capricious nature or appreciate his more creative (and arty) side. With so many hurdles, the way ahead will be difficult.

With a Monkey

The Rooster will find the Monkey a redoubtable, self-willed and sometimes crafty individual and in most situations relations between them will be poor.

In the parent–child relationship, however, the Rooster parent will be a good influence on the Monkey child, helping him to channel his energies in a focused way and allowing him to discover his strengths. There will be a good bond between them, although the Monkey's mischievous streak will sorely test the Rooster's patience.

As colleagues, there will be a lack of a rapport or trust between them. The Rooster will be particularly wary of the Monkey's opportunistic and sometimes dubious methods. As a result, they will stick to their own ways and prefer to work apart.

In love, the Rooster may be attracted by the Monkey's lively and joyful nature and, for a time, find him a fascinating companion. But the Monkey lives by his own laws and is certainly not one for the Rooster's more structured lifestyle. As both are so strong-minded and unyielding, the prospects are not good.

With another Rooster

The Rooster will quickly recognize that in another of his kind he will have met his match and, as each will want to prevail, relations will be far from easy.

In the parent–child relationship, the Rooster parent will love his Rooster child dearly and teach him a great deal. But as both have a mind of their own and are self-willed and forthright, there will be a certain edge to their relationship.

As colleagues, again their dominating personalities will show through, with each wanting to take the lead or interfering in the work of the other. In work situations, two Roosters' brash and forthright personalities just clash.

In love, they may share many interests, but again their candid natures will be their undoing. They will squabble and vie for dominance. It will take an exceptional Rooster couple to make their relationship work.

❧ With a Dog

The Dog is not as spontaneous as the Rooster and it takes time for him to get to know and trust someone. Rarely will the Rooster give the Dog that time. Relations between the two signs are poor.

In the parent–child relationship, the Rooster parent may not always appreciate just how sensitive or anxious a young Dog can be. The Dog child requires tender love, patience and gentle encouragement, and the Rooster parent, while so well meaning, may not fully appreciate the young Dog's needs. As a result, their relationship may not be the most satisfactory.

As colleagues, both may be determined to make the most of their strengths, but their styles and attitudes are very different. With little understanding or accord between them, rarely do these two work well together.

In love, the way ahead will be difficult. The Rooster will have little patience with the Dog's worrying and will aim to take charge and inject order into their home and lifestyle. But the Dog does not like to be dominated and will himself lose patience with the Rooster's exuberant style and tell him so in no uncertain terms. These two are too forthright, strong-willed and different in outlook for harmony to reign for long. A challenging match.

❧ With a Pig

The Rooster has a great admiration and respect for the Pig and relations between the two signs can be mutually beneficial.

In the parent–child relationship, the Pig child will gain much from the guidance and discipline of the Rooster parent and will strive to please. There will be a good rapport and close bond between them.

As colleagues, there is considerable respect between the Rooster and Pig and, while sometimes their approaches will differ, with the Rooster being more cautious, when working towards a specific goal they make an effective combination.

In love, these two will learn much from each other. The Rooster will especially value the Pig's positive, genial and good-natured temperament and will often become less intense as a result. They both value their home life and can have many interests, including gardening, the outdoors and socializing. These two understand and appreciate each other and make a good match.

SUCCESS IN LIFE

The Rooster is a determined and strong-willed character who likes to put himself forward. He is direct, assertive and often colourful. As a result he will do a great deal in his life, but he will need to work hard to achieve the success he desires. His life will not always be smooth and each stage will contain many lessons from which he will ultimately profit.

As a child the Rooster is keen, alert and inquisitive. He likes finding out about things and testing possibilities and this, combined with his ability to learn quickly and take in all manner of detail, will serve him well, especially in his schooling. He is also well organized, although his exacting nature, as well as his tendency to speak his mind, even at a young age, will not always go down too well with others. The young Rooster may mean well, but be too outspoken for his own good. However, with support and guidance, his formative years will be generally happy ones.

As the Rooster enters his late teens and early adulthood, his life could become more challenging. Aware of his abilities and setting himself some high expectations, he could find the progress he desires not as straightforward or even possible as he thought. At this time he will experience disappointments and some hard knocks. Some Roosters will find themselves drifting from job to job, feeling generally unfulfilled. But while this can be disheartening, all the time the Rooster will be adding to his experience and he will know that deep down he does have the ability to realize many of his aspirations. This faith in himself will help him through the early years of his working life as he starts to discover his potential.

On a personal level, these will also be significant times. A keen socializer, the Rooster will lead an active social life. While he will enjoy many romances, he will have in his mind's eye the person who will make his ideal partner. This person may take some finding, but the Rooster is prepared to wait, sometimes for years, rather than commit himself to a relationship he does not consider right.

The Rooster's middle age will be a particularly interesting phase. Although he may have started to enjoy considerable success in his work, he will still have some key goals to reach and these years will see him striving for greater success and maximizing his potential. This will be a challenging but often exciting time. Admittedly, sometimes the path the Rooster has mapped out for himself will be difficult and strewn with obstacles, but he is persistent, resourceful and meticulous in his preparation, and all this will help.

The Rooster's domestic life will also mean much to him and he will enjoy watching the progress of his partner and any children, all the time encouraging them with his positive and supportive ways. In family matters the Rooster is dutiful and conscientious.

The closing years of the Rooster's working life will often be the most fulfilling period. Having striven so hard, the Rooster will now have a role which will allow him to use his skills and years of training to good effect. He will also have the respect of many and this will mean much to him.

The Rooster's more senior years will be a contented phase. He will, as always, play an important role in family matters, doing much to advise and support his relations and taking a fond interest in any grandchildren. He will also be able to give more time to his various interests, particularly reading, gardening and the arts, as well as maintain an often busy social life. He always likes to keep active and involved and can make this a rewarding period of his life.

The Rooster's life will certainly contain many successes but, in view of his ambitious nature and high expectations, it will also contain challenges, disappointments and errors of judgement, usually caused by his outspokenness or by being too headstrong. However, the Rooster possesses a determined nature and his keenness and the faith he has in his abilities will keep him going and, despite everything, lead him to some glorious personal triumphs. The Rooster's life can indeed be an eventful and fulfilling one.

FAMOUS ROOSTERS

Francis Bacon, Enid Blyton, Sir Michael Caine, Enrico Caruso, Christopher Cazenove, Jean Chrétien, Eric Clapton, Joan Collins, Rita Coolidge, Craig David, Daniel Day Lewis, Sasha Distel, the Duke of Edinburgh, Gloria Estefan, Bryan Ferry, Errol Flynn, Benjamin Franklin, Melanie Griffith, Richard Harris, Goldie Hawn, Katharine Hepburn, Thomas H. Huxley, Diane Keaton, Søren Kierkegaard, Dean Koontz, D. H. Lawrence, David Livingstone, Ken Livingstone, Jayne Mansfield, Steve Martin, James Mason, André Maurois, Bette Midler, Van Morrison, Willie Nelson, Kim Novak, Yoko Ono, Sir William Osler, Dolly Parton, George Patton, Michelle Pfeiffer, Priscilla Presley, Joan Rivers, Jenny Seagrove, George Segal, Carly Simon, Britney Spears, Johann Strauss, Sir Peter Ustinov, Verdi, Richard Wagner, Neil Young, Catherine Zeta Jones.

SUCCESS TIPS FOR THE ROOSTER

The Rooster is an assiduous planner and wants everything to be right, but in some instances he can get embroiled in the intricacies of detail and fuss too much over the inconsequential. This can cause delay and lead him to become side-tracked. The Rooster should watch this and always keep the end result in mind. This way he is more likely to make progress. Also, he could find it helpful to set a time limit on the achievement of a certain task or activity. Again, this will help to keep him focused and moving towards what he wants.

The Rooster must also be wary of being too intransigent. Although he may map out his activities and future in great detail, situations do change. In the world of work, for instance, there is no longer the job security that there once was and it is necessary to adapt to the demands of the market-place. New positions and opportunities are being created all the time and to benefit, the Rooster *must* be prepared to be flexible. He may have his particular objectives and aspirations, but there are many routes to the top. When the situation calls for it, the Rooster must be prepared to modify his journey plan.

The Rooster thinks on a grand scale but sometimes his thoughts and ideas run away with him. Although it is important to aim high, the Rooster would find it helpful to regularly discuss his thoughts and aspirations with those able to give informed advice. By being forthcoming he will benefit from the input of others and win support for some of his objectives.

The Rooster is frank and forthright, but without consideration his words can undermine what he is hoping to achieve. As the Chinese proverb states, 'Once you have spoken, even the swiftest horses cannot retract your words.' For this reason the Rooster should think carefully before he speaks – or indeed acts.

The Rooster is very conscientious and sets himself high standards. However, he does drive himself hard and can become highly strung. In order to combat this, the Rooster would find it helpful to relax and unwind more. He should make sure he regularly devotes time to his interests, particularly those unrelated to his everyday concerns. He could find certain physical activities such as swimming, gardening, walking, yoga and *tai chi* will also help to keep him in shape and allow him to deliver his best.

SOME FINAL THOUGHTS
FROM THE ROOSTER

Perhaps the most valuable result of all education is the ability to make yourself do the thing you have to do, when it ought to be done, whether you like it or not. It is the first lesson that ought to be learned.
Thomas H. Huxley

When schemes are laid in advance, it is surprising how often the circumstances will fit in with them.
Sir William Osler

Do not squander time, for that is the stuff life is made of.
Benjamin Franklin

Never put off tomorrow what you can do today.
Benjamin Franklin

To be gentle, tolerant, wise and reasonable requires a goodly portion on toughness.
Sir Peter Ustinov

If I were to wish for anything, I should not wish for wealth and power, but for the passionate sense of the potential, for the eye which, ever young and ardent, sees the possible ... what wine is so sparkling, so fragrant, so intoxicating, as possibility!
Søren Kierkegaard

Life is not a problem to be solved but a reality to be experienced.
Søren Kierkegaard

Take calculated risks. That is different from being rash.
George Patton

A wise man will make more opportunities than he finds.
Francis Bacon

If you create an act, you create a habit. If you create a habit you create a character. If you create a character, you create destiny.
André Maurois

The
Dog

Whether as a mountain rescuer, pulling sleighs, guarding property or being a family pet, the Dog is a good and loyal friend to man. Dutiful, hard-working and affectionate, the Dog can be depended upon and these features are so often found in those born under the eleventh Chinese sign.

The Dog has a particularly caring nature. He is not only loyal and protective towards those who are important to him, but he also speaks out against any wrongs or injustices that he sees. The Dog is very much the champion of good causes and many Dogs will give time to charitable work, helping others or campaigning for some issue. When motivated or rankled by some cause, the call to action will be just too strong for the Dog to ignore.

It is because he possesses such a noble heart and is prepared to stand his ground that the Dog is so well regarded by others. He inspires respect and confidence and those around him will often set much store by his judgement.

The Dog is a no-nonsense sort of character. He does not hedge, but is open with his views and he speaks as he finds. If he considers something is wrong, he can be critical and blunt. Similarly, in his relations with others, if someone should say or do something he disagrees with, he will soon let his feelings be known. With the Dog, you know exactly where you stand. He does not prevaricate.

The Dog also possesses a keen and lively mind. He is quick to appraise situations and relies on intuition and instinct. He does, though, tend to view things in black and white and once he has made up his mind, he is not one to change it easily. He is a deep thinker and often dwells on his current situation and the consequences of any action he may be considering. As a result, he is a worrier.

The Dog is actually born under the signs of loyalty and anxiety, and anxiety is one of the chief factors that can undermine his level of success. By analysing situations, he can sometimes imagine the worst. Anxiety can gnaw away at him, undermining his confidence as well as his relations with those around him. So many Dogs are anxious and pessimistic, and they would do well to try to conquer these tendencies. Instead of thinking the worst, they should focus on the positive, on what is going right for them and what they can be thankful for. Also, rather than dwell so much on mistakes, setbacks and rebuffs (which we all have), instead they should think of past successes and achievements. Unless checked, worry, depression and melancholy can spoil so much for the Dog and he should try to overcome this side of his personality. He has many fine qualities and should build on these rather than dwell on the negative. Sir Winston Churchill, himself a Dog, once commented, 'When I look back on all these worries I remember the story of the old man who said on his deathbed that he had had a lot of trouble in his life, most of which never happened.'

An effective way for the Dog to counter his worrying tendencies is for him to absorb himself in his work and his various pursuits. He needs to keep occupied and be involved in activities with purpose, ideally those that can help others. The Dog does like to serve and when he is doing something that counts, he is at his best.

In his work, the Dog makes a particularly good team member. Always keen to do his share, he is loyal to his colleagues and maintains high standards. He takes his responsibilities seriously and his judgement, integrity and openness are much appreciated. The Dog may not be as ambitious as some, but his willingness to learn and his specialist talents will take him far. Unlike some, the Dog is not particularly driven by financial considerations. He will take more pleasure in knowing that what he is doing is of value to others. Of all the Chinese signs, the Dog is the most unselfish and altruistic.

As he is such a fine and dependable worker, the Dog certainly has the ability to earn a good income. He can be most generous with his money, as he can with his time, especially towards his family, close friends and those he feels have an especial need.

However, although he is so well regarded, the Dog is not an easy socializer. He dislikes large gatherings, exchanging small talk with those he hardly knows or putting on false airs. Rather than build up a large number of acquaintants, he prefers to have a smaller social circle and a few really good and loyal friends. Indeed, he does choose his friends with care, letting his friendships develop gradually on a basis of trust and understanding. When someone has won his confidence – which again takes time – the Dog will be a dependable and loyal friend. The friendship of the Dog is something to be treasured.

Similarly, when falling in love, the Dog does take time before committing himself to another. He needs to feel at ease and be certain of his own feelings before he can place his trust in someone else. Sometimes his hesitancy as well as his tendency to analyse can undermine a promising romance, but once he has found someone to share his life with, the Dog makes a caring and faithful partner. As with so much of his life, he will take the relationship and the responsibilities it brings with it very seriously. If he becomes a parent, he will be devoted and attentive to his children and endeavour to give them all they need. While he may be a good disciplinarian, his children will also be aware of his softer side and will have a way of getting round him! The Dog does indeed possess a warm and kindly heart.

The male Dog is quieter than the female and more of a loner. He holds strong views and once he is inspired by a goal, he will work tirelessly to achieve it. At times he can be stubborn and difficult and prone to worry, but his determination and strong sense of fair play, as well as his loyalty towards others, make him someone who is both respected and loved.

The female Dog is more sociable and outgoing. Although she too builds up friendships slowly and carefully, she is generally more at ease with others and when in company she likes, she can be a witty and lively speaker. She likes to keep herself active and while her partner and family will always be her priority, she does maintain a good range of outside interests. She sets high standards and, in keeping with the Dog personality, can be especially critical of those who do not meet her expectations. In appearance, she prefers practical and casual clothes to anything too ornate. Neither is she particularly bothered by the latest in fashion. She knows what she likes and chooses accordingly.

Both the male and female Dog attach considerable importance to their home and will keep it tidy and well organized. While the Dog may have conservative tastes and is rarely impressed by new gadgets or fads, his home will be thoughtfully furnished and well maintained.

As far as his personal interests are concerned, the Dog does like to keep himself physically active. Some Dogs will be particularly keen on sport, while others will enjoy pursuits such as gardening, dancing, walking or something similar which keeps them out and about. With his practical nature, the Dog also enjoys making things and could obtain much pleasure from some sort of craft or from carrying out practical projects on his home or from the culinary arts.

Those Dogs who are born during the day are considered to have a generally calmer disposition than those born at night, but with their caring and dependable nature, their integrity and unwavering loyalty towards those who mean so much to them, all Dogs have many worthy traits. If the Dog can overcome his tendency to worry, then he will find his life both easier and more pleasurable as a result. And during his life he will enjoy some wonderful achievements as well as win the gratitude and admiration of many.

SUCCESS AND WORK

The Dog needs to feel that what he does has value and when this is applied to his work, he can be an inspiration to others. Dedicated, assiduous and always willing to play a part, he is a tireless worker. In addition he is loyal, trustworthy and makes a fine and active team member.

When the Dog is motivated, his drive and sense of purpose are such that he can, if he chooses, move quite swiftly towards more senior positions. He certainly has the abilities and tenacity to go far. However, with every job he takes on, it is so important that he feels he is playing a useful role. If he becomes disenchanted with his position, then he could find himself starting to drift, becoming prone to bouts of pessimism and depression and certainly not making the most of his abilities. The Dog has to believe that what he does is worthwhile.

It is for this reason that the Dog should choose his own vocation. Sometimes parental pressure or influence from others could direct him into the wrong type of work or, if suitable positions are hard to obtain, he may be forced to take on an unfulfilling role. If he does feel this way, then he owes it to himself to try for something more in line with what *he* wants to do. Inspired and motivated, the Dog can rise to great heights. Uninspired and disenchanted, he can become a sorry figure.

In view of his desire to serve, the Dog can often find fulfilment in the medical or caring professions, while his desire for justice will be fulfilled in the police force and legal professions. The Dog can also make a good adviser, social or community worker, psychologist and teacher. Some Dogs will be called to the Church. The Dog's desire to champion causes and fight injustice can make him an inspired politician or campaigner. He is also prepared to specialize and his expertise and mastery of facts can propel him into responsible positions.

Whatever career the Dog chooses, once he feels inspired and motivated, he is certainly capable of making an impression and playing an important role. He is not motivated by financial gain, but by the value of what he does. Indeed, the world of commerce, aggressive marketing and speculation does little for him. Once he has found his true calling and feels fulfilled, that is reward enough.

SUCCESS AND MONEY

The Dog is one of the few signs that is not particularly concerned about money. As long as his needs are covered and that he can provide for his loved ones, then he will be content. Money, to him, is a useful and necessary tool but it does not preoccupy or particularly inspire him. To the Dog, there are far more important and valuable purposes in life than to be continually driven by the need to acquire and accumulate.

However, while money is rarely a motivating factor, the Dog's abilities and keenness to work ensure that he is capable of earning a good income and satisfying both his own needs and those of his loved ones. The Dog can be particularly generous towards family members and, as ever, will help and support them as much as he can. He is a good and conscientious provider and sometimes gets more pleasure from spending on his loved ones than on himself. Should he ever find himself with money to spare, then he does not always put it to its best use and will often be tempted to spend it quite freely.

However, while the Dog may not be overly interested in money matters, he should still aim to build up his assets, either for when he may have some heavy expenses or for his longer-term future. He could find it helpful to take out a regular savings plan and could also benefit from the savings and tax allowances that are often available. While he may not feel comfortable with certain forms of speculation or risk-taking, by saving with a reputable company and in a scheme with a good track record, he can in time build up a useful reserve.

In money matters the Dog does need to give some thought to the preservation of what he has as well as make provision for the future. This is, after all, too important to ignore or leave to chance. While not necessarily seeking great wealth, if the Dog takes the time and effort to manage his money, he is capable of enjoying a comfortable and secure lifestyle.

SUCCESS AND LOVE

The Dog has an affectionate and caring nature and makes a most attentive partner. But finding his soulmate is not an easy process for him. It does take the Dog some considerable time before he feels at ease with another. At first he can appear reserved and distant and his general attitude can prevent many a promising romance from getting underway.

However, before committing himself to another, the Dog does need to get to know that person well and throughout the early stages of any romance he will spend much time thinking over conversations and the general attitude of the other person. Sometimes, if that person does not meet the Dog's ideals or becomes impatient with his attitude, the romance is likely to flounder. And the Dog himself does not make the process any easier. Although he obviously wants to pick the right partner, to constantly analyse the relationship could prevent him from enjoying it as much as he otherwise could, as well as bring him yet more worry. The Dog needs to relax and let love happen rather than be so cautious and analytical.

However, once the Dog has found a person to love, he will be passionate and caring and certainly give his all to make the relationship work. But in return his partner will need to frequently reassure him and help lift him from his sometimes anxious and despondent states. The Dog needs someone who will understand him, cope with his mood swings and support and encourage him in his activities. Ideally, his partner should be someone who is more outgoing and possesses a lively as well as considerate nature. The Dog is not the easiest person to live with, but he is dependable, takes his commitment seriously and will be a loyal and loving friend and partner.

Falling in love and committing himself to a relationship takes a long time for the Dog, but his life will be so much richer when he has someone to love.

SUCCESS WITH OTHERS

The Dog is very direct in his dealings with others. He is not one for idle chatter or inane pleasantries, but instead comes straight to the point and speaks his mind. It also takes him some while before he feels at ease with another. As Robert Louis Stevenson, a Dog, once wrote, 'A friend is a present you give yourself.' The Dog chooses his presents carefully. However, while the Dog's manner may sometimes appear abrupt, he is much admired for his sincerity, loyalty and dependability. In his relations with others he will, though, find he is able to enjoy a greater rapport with some signs than others.

With a Rat

Lively, outgoing and so full of charm, the Rat is much admired by the Dog and these two can strike up a good rapport.

In the parent–child relationship, the Rat child will thrive under the guidance of an attentive and caring Dog parent. Being so quick on the uptake and having such a lively and resourceful spirit, the young Rat will give the Dog parent good reason to feel proud. There will be a close and loving bond between them.

As colleagues, relations will not be so easy. In business the Rat is enterprising, ambitious and keen to make the most of situations, and his opportunistic and materialistic approach does not always sit comfortably with the more idealistic Dog. As a result, each will feel hindered by the other and in work situations they do not make a successful combination.

In love, however, their different personalities complement each other and both will benefit from the relationship. The Dog will value the Rat's optimistic and affectionate nature and as both value their home life and make attentive parents, this too

will draw them closer together. Admittedly their different attitudes towards housekeeping, with the Rat being far more thrifty
than the Dog, will need to be reconciled, but these two are well
suited.

With an Ox

The Dog may admire the Ox's open and down-to-earth manner,
but these two are redoubtable characters and will not feel at
ease in each other's company.

In the parent–child relationship, the Dog parent could
worry much over the Ox child's quiet and withdrawn manner,
not always realizing the young Ox prefers to be left to his
own devices. Misunderstandings between them could be quite
common.

As colleagues, both may be hard and dutiful workers, but
their forthright natures will soon get the better of them. The Dog
will find it hard to accept the Ox's assertive and sometimes
unyielding manner and as a result there will often be a lack of
understanding between them.

In love, both possess cautious natures and like to allow time
for any relationship to develop. But for a relationship between
these two signs to work, a good deal of care and understanding
will be needed. The Dog will value the Ox's sincere and dependable manner, but could find he is not always as sensitive or
understanding as he may like. As both can be stubborn and
speak their minds, there could be some tricky periods. In love
they are not particularly suited.

With the Tiger

The lively, sincere and good-natured ways of the Tiger greatly
appeal to the Dog and these two can become firm friends. As

both are idealists and enjoy supporting humanitarian causes, they could find they have much in common.

In the parent–child relationship, there will be an excellent understanding between Dog parent and Tiger child, with the Dog providing the right level of support and discipline for the young Tiger and helping him to master his sometimes restless nature. There will be much love between them.

As colleagues, these two trust each other and will benefit from their individual strengths. The Dog will feel particularly inspired by the Tiger's openness, integrity (both are very ethical in their dealings) and wealth of ideas. They will each contribute a great deal to their work and together they make a successful team.

In love, the Dog and Tiger are well suited. The Dog will draw comfort from the supportive ways of the Tiger, feeling that he is someone who understands and cares. In addition he will admire the Tiger's lively and genial nature and generous spirit. These two have many interests they can share and each will learn much from the other. This can be a happy match.

With a Rabbit

The Dog has a great admiration for the quiet, refined and discreet ways of the Rabbit and relations between them will be good.

In the parent–child relationship, the generally quiet and well-behaved Rabbit child will strive to please the Dog parent and they will enjoy a close and meaningful rapport.

As colleagues, their respect and mutual trust can make for a rewarding partnership. Both are honourable in their business dealings and are willing to pool their individual strengths and work hard. Problems will only come if any serious setbacks or developments occur, as neither copes well under stress or great pressure. But when circumstances are in their favour, these two will go from strength to strength.

In love, they are well suited. As both seek a secure and stable existence and often have similar interests and tastes, there is a good understanding between them. The Dog will admire the generally serene and kindly Rabbit and will value having such a loyal, reliable and supportive partner. These two can become very devoted to each other and make a successful match.

With a Dragon

The Dragon may have a lively and outgoing personality but his style does not impress the Dog. Relations between the two will be poor.

In the parent–child relationship, the Dog parent will find the spirited and independent-minded ways of a young Dragon something of a trial. The Dog parent will do much to love, support and guide the Dragon child, but relations between them will often be tricky.

As colleagues, these two will soon clash. Both are straight talkers, both will try to prevail and the Dog will be scornful of the Dragon's impulsive and, to his mind, ill-considered approach. They will soon go their separate ways.

In love, this could be a challenging match. Although the Dog could benefit from having such a lively and self-assured partner, their often different interests and outlooks will be difficult to reconcile. As both can be stubborn, like to dominate and speak their minds, the prospects are not good.

With a Snake

The Dog admires the quiet and thoughtful Snake and as both take their time in building up relations, their cautious and reserved natures will suit them both. These two get on well.

In the parent–child relationship, the Snake child will thrive in a Dog household, appreciating the attention, love and care the Dog parent will bestow. There will be a good bond and a great deal of respect between them.

As colleagues, they may respect each other but their different outlooks do not make for a particularly effective combination. The Dog likes to be part of a team and needs to feel inspired, but the Snake is more of a self-starter and, in work matters, does not particularly enthuse the Dog.

In love, the Dog and Snake mean much to each other, with the Dog especially valuing the Snake's calm, considerate and positive nature. Admittedly there will be some differences they will need to reconcile and the Dog will not feel entirely comfortable with the Snake's more materialistic streak, but with care and understanding these two can make a close and meaningful match.

With a Horse

The Dog likes the lively and high-spirited Horse and relations between the two signs will be good.

In the parent–child relationship, the Dog will do much to encourage the young Horse in his many interests and activities. While the Horse child's independent and spirited ways will sometimes concern the Dog parent, there will be much love between them.

As colleagues, the Dog and Horse make a successful combination, with the Dog admiring the Horse's industry as well as finding him an encouraging and inspirational colleague. These two work well together and by combining their different strengths can go far.

In love, the Dog and Horse are well suited, with the Dog especially appreciating the Horse's lively and positive nature. They share many interests, in particular outdoor activities, and could be keen travellers, gardeners or sports enthusiasts. The Horse is good for the Dog, as he will be supportive and help to dispel some of the Dog's worries. They can make an excellent match.

With a Goat

The Dog finds it hard to relate to the whimsical and capricious Goat and relations between the two signs are poor.

In the parent–child relationship, the young Goat will treasure the love and care of a Dog parent, but as their interests and outlooks do not always coincide, their understanding and rapport may not always be the greatest.

As colleagues, the Goat and Dog do not work well together. To be at their best, both need to feel motivated and inspired, but instead these two will antagonize each other. The Dog will be particularly critical of the Goat's more laid-back style and not always appreciate his more imaginative approach.

In love, the Dog may recognize the Goat's kindly and good-natured ways, but the prospects are bleak. The Dog will soon become exasperated by the Goat's capriciousness and his own direct manner will often upset the Goat's sensitivities. With both being prone to worry and having such different outlooks, theirs will be a challenging match.

With a Monkey

At first sight the Dog may care little for the lively and quick-witted Monkey, but once he gets to know him better, he will learn a great deal from him and the two can form a beneficial relationship.

In the parent–child relationship, the Dog parent will do much to encourage the Monkey child and will be especially pleased with his versatility and quickness to learn. However, he may not be so appreciative of the young Monkey's more mischievous and artful ways.

As colleagues, if they are sufficiently inspired and working towards a common goal, the Dog and Monkey can combine their different strengths to good effect. In such a situation, the Dog will particularly value the Monkey's enthusiastic and enterprising approach. However, to be at their best, these two do need to focus on something specific.

In love, the Dog and Monkey complement each other, with both gaining much from their relationship. The Monkey's optimistic and good-hearted nature will be good for the Dog and he can also broaden the Dog's outlook. As these two get to know each other better, they will be drawn closer and can find much happiness together.

With a Rooster

As both signs are strong-willed and speak their minds, it will not be too long before their forthright natures get the better of them. Relations between the Rooster and Dog are generally poor.

In the parent–child relationship, the Dog parent will admire the Rooster child's keen and conscientious nature, but the young Rooster is self-willed and could give the Dog parent some worrying times. The Dog parent does want to help, but the Rooster child may not always be as receptive as the Dog may wish.

As colleagues, there is little empathy between Dog and Rooster. The Rooster wants to organize and be in control and the

Dog will resist his domineering attitude. As both are outspoken, there will be almost constant tension between them.

In love, the way ahead will be fraught with difficulty. Although the Dog may admire the Rooster's lively and well-meaning nature, the Rooster likes to impose his structured lifestyle on others and the Dog will resent this. Nor will the Dog care for the Rooster's self-centred and pernickety ways and as both are forthright and stand their ground, their different views will soon and frequently be aired. A difficult match.

With another Dog

With similar values and outlooks, two Dogs together get on well. There is a good understanding and rapport between them.

In the parent–child relationship the Dog parent, being so aware of the concerns of a young Dog, will do much to support and encourage him as well as provide the love the Dog child so needs. The young Dog will thrive under such care and this will be a close and special relationship.

As colleagues, two Dogs will respect each other but may not be the most effective combination. As the Dog can be prone to worry and is not the most commercially minded of signs, two Dogs' talents and potential could go untapped.

In love, there will be a great bond and understanding between two Dogs. They will be supportive of each other and will often share interests. They both value their home life and make attentive parents. Their forthright natures will, though, sometimes clash and at difficult times both could get despondent. Nevertheless, these two will depend on each other and their love will be strong and enduring. A successful match.

With a Pig

The Dog likes the genial and easy-going Pig and relations between the two signs are good.

In the parent–child relationship, the Pig child will respond well to the firm but loving guidance of the Dog and the Dog will gain from having such a bright and cheerful member in his household. There will be much love between them.

As colleagues, the Dog and Pig make an effective combination, with the Dog often being inspired by the earnest and hard-working Pig. Both attach much importance to business ethics and to being open and honourable in their dealings. By joining forces and combining their skills, they can enjoy considerable success.

In love, the Dog and Pig can find much happiness. They share several common interests, including a love of the outdoors, and both have strong humanitarian leanings. The Dog will appreciate the Pig's more optimistic nature as well as his ability to understand and empathize. These two are good for each other and can make a splendid match.

SUCCESS THROUGH LIFE

When the Dog is inspired and feels that what he is doing is of value, then he is capable of going far and achieving much. He is a hard worker, honourable in his dealings with others and has a caring nature. He has so much to give. However, his life is very much affected by his feelings, as he is so prone to anxiety. If he can conquer this or at least cope with his bleaker moods, then his life will be much happier and more successful as a result.

The Dog's childhood years are especially important and if he is brought up in a supportive and loving atmosphere, then this can help him a great deal in later life. In these formative years he needs encouragement and care and to feel confident and at ease with himself. If, in his childhood, he lacks the attention and support he needs, then he could withdraw into himself and become moody, starting a pattern which he will frequently have to battle to break. How the young Dog fares academically will also be coloured by his feelings. Again, if he feels inspired and encouraged he could excel, but if not he could become anxious and pessimistic and fall behind.

As he moves into his late teens and early adult years, the Dog will be keen to prove himself and demonstrate to others (and himself) his true worth. Admittedly, as he ventures forward, he will again go through many anxious periods, but employers will soon identify his keen spirit and conscientious nature and the Dog will be quick to make an impact. When he has identified the work he likes or company he feels comfortable working for, then he will not be keen to change. The Dog likes security and stability. He likes to build up his expertise and this too will help him to advance.

On a personal level, the Dog's early adult years could see him grappling with the complexities of love. While so eager to find someone to share his life with, he needs time to build a satisfying and close relationship. A romance which does not work out may likewise take him some while to recover from. He so wants to find love, but finding Mr or Ms Right can be a long and often anxious process.

When he does settle down, the Dog will be keenly aware of his responsibilities both to his partner and to any children. His attentiveness towards them will often lead him to worry about any problems they might have or whether he is doing his best for them. As always, the Dog is keenly aware of both his own situation and of those who mean so much to him. But the time he devotes to setting up his home will bring him a great deal of pleasure.

In his work, the Dog's loyalty and expertise will often serve him well and his middle years can see him making significant advances. If he does find himself in an unfulfilling role or having to look for another job, he should draw on his strength and resolve and persist until he has found something suitable. He has so much to offer that he owes it to himself (and dependants) to use his skills to good effect.

As he passes into older age, the Dog should continue to occupy himself with worthwhile activities and interests. These could be helping family members, furthering his existing interests or involving himself in some sort of charity or community work. By continuing to contribute, the Dog can make this a satisfying time.

In their later years many Dogs will also find themselves dwelling on the course of their life, thinking perhaps of chances missed or what might have happened had they acted differently. Again, so many choose to dwell on the negative and so cloud their later years. But with all he has achieved, the people he has helped, the successes he has enjoyed and the happy times he has had, the Dog is bound to have had a life that has been both eventful *and* fulfilling.

FAMOUS DOGS

Henry Brook Adams, King Albert II of Belgium, Brigette Bardot, Candice Bergen, David Bowie, Bertolt Brecht, George W. Bush, Mariah Carey, King Carl Gustaf XVI of Sweden, José Carreras, Paul Cézanne, Cher, The Earl of Chesterfield, Sir Winston Churchill, Bill Clinton, Leonard Cohen, Jamie Lee Curtis, Claude Debussy, Dame Judi Dench, Blake Edwards, Sally Field, Joseph Fiennes, Robert Frost, Ava Gardner, Judy Garland, George Gershwin, William Hazlitt, Victor Hugo, Barry Humphries,

Holly Hunter, Michael Jackson, Al Jolson, David Lloyd George, Jennifer Lopez, Sophia Loren, Shirley MacLaine, Madonna, Norman Mailer, Barry Manilow, Freddie Mercury, Liza Minnelli, David Niven, Elvis Presley, Paul Robeson, Susan Sarandon, Claudia Schiffer, Dr Albert Schweitzer, Sylvester Stallone, Robert Louis Stevenson, Sharon Stone, Chris Tarrant, Mother Teresa, Uma Thurman, Anthony Trollope, Voltaire, Prince William, Shelley Winters.

SUCCESS TIPS FOR THE DOG

The Dog is a worrier and does get anxious about a great deal. Rather than dwell on his concerns by himself, he should be prepared to share his troubles with those close to him. Often others will be pleased to help and advise as well as have the chance to return the Dog's own many kindnesses. It has so often been said that a worry shared is a worry halved and the Dog must always remember this. Also, at worrying times, he could find it helpful to keep himself occupied, particularly with interests he enjoys. As the Chinese proverb states, 'One joy scatters one hundred griefs.' And some of the Dog's interests can be real joys.

Once the Dog has made up his mind, he is not one to change it. His opinions stick fast and he does tend to view things in black and white. However, in some situations, it would certainly be in his interests to be more flexible. Sometimes circumstances change, new information comes to light or unexpected opportunities emerge. The Dog must be open to these and prepared to adapt. Sometimes his intransigence can prevent him from moving on as swiftly as he otherwise might and in certain situations it really would be beneficial for him to show a greater flexibility.

The Dog possesses a highly practical nature and is capable of coming up with some excellent ideas. However, he may often do nothing about them and be dismissive about their prospects. Instead, he should have faith in them. The Dog has a practical approach as well as often considerable experience, and his ideas could strike a positive response. He owes it to himself to put them forward and see what results. It is those who push forward who move forward.

To succeed also requires continual development and every so often the Dog should make a conscious effort to broaden his horizons, maybe learning a new skill, extending an interest or reading up about another subject. Whatever he does, furthering his knowledge will benefit him as well as bring him much personal satisfaction.

Our thoughts are so vital to our well-being, but sometimes the Dog's thoughts tend towards the negative and so have an inhibiting effect upon his outlook and resolve. Whenever he has more negative thoughts, he should try some positive self-talk instead. As a man thinks, so he becomes, and by changing his thoughts, the Dog can really improve his attitude and prospects. As Emile Coué taught his students, regular repetition of the statement, 'Every day, and in every way, I am becoming better and better' can have a marked effect.

The Dog has so many admirable qualities that in his life he should go forward with determination *and* a positive spirit. He will find his life so much happier and more fulfilling as a result.

SOME FINAL THOUGHTS FROM DOGS

Firmness of purpose is one of the most necessary sinews of character, and one of the best instruments of success.
The Earl of Chesterfield

Whatever is worth doing at all is worth doing well.
The Earl of Chesterfield

Each player must accept the cards life deals him or her.
But once they are in hand, he or she alone must decide how to
play the cards in order to win the game.
Voltaire

All experience is an arch to build upon.
Henry Brook Adams

I believe in an ultimate decency of things.
Robert Louis Stevenson

To travel hopefully is a better thing than to arrive, and the true
success is to labour.
Robert Louis Stevenson

Don't be afraid to take a big step if one is indicated. You can't
cross a chasm in two small jumps.
David Lloyd George

The price of greatness is responsibility.
Sir Winston Churchill

We make a living by what we get, we make a life by what we
give.
Sir Winston Churchill

It is no use saying, 'We are doing our best.' You have to succeed
in doing what is necessary.
Sir Winston Churchill

Above all things, never think that you're not good enough
yourself. A man should never think that. My belief is that in life
people will take you very much at your own reckoning.
Anthony Trollope

If you think you can win, you can win. Faith is necessary to
victory.
William Hazlitt

The
Pig

According to legend the Pig was the last animal to arrive at the Buddha's party and so the last to have a year named in his honour. Those born under the twelfth Chinese sign are blessed with some fine and noble qualities.

Pigs are born under the sign of honesty and are sincere and generous with a great sense of fun. They enjoy life and not only make great company but are also well respected.

The Pig possesses a good heart. When others are in need, are facing problems or have experienced some bad news, the Pig is the ideal person to offer comfort and support. He knows how to empathize and listen and because of this makes a valuable friend.

With his genial nature the Pig also makes an effective peace-maker and arbiter of disputes. He has a particular dislike of arguments and bickering and will do his utmost to calm an awkward situation. In some cases, he may even turn a blind eye to certain things if it makes life easier.

The Pig is certainly easy-going and tolerant, but this does not mean he is without strength of character. He is hard-working and resolute and can often achieve considerable success and wealth. When his mind is made up about something, he can be stubborn and obstinate. However, he is dependable and when he takes on a commitment he is almost certain to see it through. He does not like unfinished business and, being true to his word, takes his obligations seriously.

The Pig works hard, but he plays hard too. He possesses a good sense of humour, although for some this can verge on the coarse and bawdy. He greatly enjoys his food and drink and enjoys socializing. He will have a wide social circle drawn from many walks of life. Admittedly at some social functions the Pig may feel ill at ease, particularly if he has to talk in front of large numbers or if the occasion is highly formal and the Pig is anxious to do no wrong. However, when he is in more relaxed situations and the food and drink are flowing freely, he will often come into his own. Witty, lively and talkative, he can easily become the focus of attention and sometimes the source of much merriment.

The Pig certainly has many great qualities and with his capacity to work hard and to deliver results, he can achieve a great deal. However, the road to success will not be easy and the Pig will have to learn some hard and sometimes painful lessons. In particular, he can be naïve and has a tendency to take things at face value. Sometimes this can lead to mistakes and those less scrupulous may take advantage of the Pig's trusting nature. In some situations he would do well to be more discerning.

Also, the Pig is not that good a planner. He is very much focused on the present and does not tend to give too much thought to the longer term. As a result he can miss out on opportunities or not make as much of himself as he otherwise might. If the Pig were to think ahead and set himself some longer term objectives to work towards, he could find his achievements that much greater.

In addition, being the great pleasure-seeker that he is, the Pig does run the risk of becoming over-indulgent. Sometimes, if he has had too much to drink (and the Pig does not tend to hold his liquor well) he can embarrass others by being too blunt or bawdy. And should he experience any serious setback or bad news, then there is a real risk that he could let himself go, perhaps by starting to drink more than is good for him and so setting himself on a downward spiral. The Pig does need to be mindful of the risks of over-indulgence and excess.

However, while life will teach the Pig some painful lessons, he is robust and resilient, a true survivor. Many a Pig has gone on to achieve great success after experiencing some setback or misfortune, having learnt from the lessons life has taught him. Indeed, some Pigs will find that a setback is the trigger they need to bring out their best qualities and make them really strive for what they want.

Also, the Pig will enjoy a good level of support throughout his life. Due to his decency and integrity, he instils trust and is well liked. He should always remember that if he does ever have any concerns, there are many he can turn to for advice. They will be pleased to reciprocate the many kindnesses the Pig has himself offered.

As far as his more personal relations are concerned, the Pig has a warm and passionate nature. He is, after all, a pleasure-seeker and not only possesses a strong libido but also delights in company. His appetite for life and sense of fun certainly make him popular and he will often have many admirers. While Pigs can be promiscuous in their early adult years, once they do find a partner with whom they wish to settle down, they will be loyal and strive for a settled and harmonious home life. Again, the Pig's desire for an easy-going and stable existence will be paramount.

As far as the actual home is concerned, some Pig homes will be totally disorganized, while others will be pristine, but all will possess a warm and welcoming feel. And with the Pig's delight in entertaining and socializing, the food and drinks cupboards will almost always be well stocked!

The Pig revels in parenthood, particularly the Pig mother, who has so much love to give her young. With his generous nature, the Pig is apt to spoil his children. However, he is a good teacher and, despite his easy-going manner, makes an effective disciplinarian, with the result that children often thrive in his care.

The male Pig is more outgoing than the female and has a genial and lively disposition. He likes to keep himself active and in addition to his tendency to work hard, he will greatly enjoy his domestic life, especially carrying out practical activities around his home. He is often a keen do-it-yourself enthusiast. He also likes his pleasures, especially good food and drink. In appearance the male Pig can be quite distinguished and sometimes will have a certain feature about his apparel that will get him noticed. Whether it is a tendency to wear particularly bright and colourful shirts, distinctive ties or some other distinguishing feature, the male can, when he wants, make himself look distinctive.

The female Pig possesses a warm and caring nature and is especially attentive towards her loved ones. Her family and home are very much her priority and she will support, advise, love and mother those closest to her. Like the male, she has a practical nature and often enjoys making things for the home or even clothes for herself and her family. She is both adept and resourceful. She also possesses a great sense of fun and enjoys entertaining and having friends round for a meal and chat. Indeed, she much prefers these sorts of occasions, when she can be herself and in company she knows and likes, to larger and more formal groups. The female Pig can also be particularly attractive in her appearance, choosing her clothes well and possessing a good sense of style and colour.

Both the male and female like carrying out practical activities and as far as leisure interests are concerned, they enjoy those that allow them to be creative. The Pig can often be skilled in a particular craft and get much pleasure from making various items. In addition, with his fondness for food, he can be an adventurous cook. He could even enjoy growing some of the food he prepares. The Pig is a keen reader and interested in the world of entertainment. He could particularly enjoy watching television and films or going out to live entertainment. Some Pigs may themselves be drawn into the performing arts and, whether in amateur dramatics or performing in some other way, with his *joie de vivre* and sense of fun the Pig can greatly enjoy himself – and often impress!

The Pig will indeed lead a full and eventful life. Although it is considered less fortunate for Pigs to be born around the start of the Chinese year, all Pigs, with their genial nature and kindly ways, will play an important part in the lives of many. The Pig enjoys life and has much energy and love to give. Wherever he goes and whatever he does, he will be an important and valued presence.

SUCCESS AND WORK

The Pig enjoys a comfortable lifestyle and he realizes that to achieve it he will need to work hard and apply himself. Accordingly, he is a conscientious worker and will always carry out his duties with care and on time. In work the Pig sets high standards and delivers results. He is prepared to work well beyond the call of duty in order to meet his obligations. Unlike some, who may be tempted to abandon activities halfway through, the Pig takes satisfaction in seeing commitments through to the end. His reliability means he will rarely find himself out of work.

The Pig cares a lot about his reputation and with his conscientious nature and ability to get on so well with others, he is invariably well regarded by his colleagues. However, while he can achieve a good level of success in his chosen line of work, he is not as competitive as some. As a result he may lose out on promotion because he does not put himself forward or lacks the competitive edge or special sparkle that can make all the difference at an interview. But the Pig is very much a 'take me as you find me' sort of character and it is often his dependable and down-to-earth qualities that enable him to make the progress he does.

When starting out on a career many Pigs do not know what they really want to do and tend to drift from position to position. Sometimes the Pig's early working life can be troubled by uncertainties, disappointment and disillusionment. For those who do decide to put themselves forward and take some risks, there could be some painful setbacks and hard lessons. However, the seeds of success are so often sown during adversity and a great many Pigs will learn well from their experiences and realize that if they are to make the most of themselves it will be through their *own* efforts. Certainly, with resolve and determination the Pig can set himself on course for some great achievements. Some of the most successful Pigs have only won through after a very difficult start.

In his choice of career, the Pig is best suited to positions which allow him to work with others. He can often make a good teacher, doctor, social worker or carer. With his practical skills, he could also be attracted to design and technical work or a specialist craft. His love of books and broad knowledge can also make him an effective researcher or writer, while the excitement and glamour of show business and the performing arts can attract some Pigs to the world of entertainment. With his fondness of food the Pig can be a fine chef or caterer. He also possesses considerable commercial acumen and can make a shrewd and often successful businessperson.

Whatever type of work the Pig chooses, he has the commitment to do well. And while not all Pigs may have the desire to reach the greatest heights of their profession, as long as the Pig feels that he is giving his best, obtaining satisfaction from what he does *and* earning a good living, he will be content.

SUCCESS AND MONEY

Although the Pig may not always admit it, money is very important to him. He likes to live well and he works hard so that he can play hard. And he does so enjoy the fruits of his labour!

The Pig is a big spender. He has expensive tastes and always looks for quality, even though it will cost him more. Also, when he goes out enjoying himself, he will often be very generous. With the Pig, money does flow freely.

However, while the Pig is certainly one to enjoy his money, he can be quite canny in financial matters. He can be a shrewd investor, sensing out companies whose share price is about to outperform or putting his money in schemes which offer a good return. He may spend his money freely, but he also knows where money is to be made. Should he experience misfortune, once he has sorted himself out (which can take some time), he will work hard to recover his fortunes and build up his wealth. In this he can be most successful. And having once tasted misfortune, he will resolve never to let it happen again.

As a good standard of living is so important to the Pig, he does take a keen interest in his financial situation. However, to avoid mistakes, it would be worth him taking particular care when entering into financial commitments. His inclination to take things at face value can lead to mistakes and his trusting nature can make him a victim of scams and confidence tricksters. In some situations the Pig can be gullible and he does need to watch this. Also, he can yield to temptation all too readily and on some occasions a little more forethought or prudence would not come amiss.

However, through hard work, determination and a fair amount of good fortune, the Pig is invariably successful in earning a good living and enjoying the wealth that he creates.

SUCCESS AND LOVE

With his charm, generous spirit and kindly nature, the Pig makes a popular companion. He is easy-going, has a ready wit and is prepared to listen to others. As a result, he will win the hearts of many. And he does so enjoy the thrills and passions of love.

Before he settles down the Pig is likely to enjoy many passionate romances, throwing himself wholeheartedly into each relationship and enjoying the excitement of love. When the Pig is deeply in love his whole being is affected, so much so that he may be found wandering around starry-eyed, thinking of little else but his loved one. Should the romance fail, he will, for a time, be traumatized and fall into a pool of despondency. The Pig needs someone to love and when he loses this, his confidence and self-esteem can take a hard knock.

However, while the path of true love does not always run smooth and the Pig could be hurt on several occasions, when he does settle down with a partner he will usually choose wisely. Of all the Chinese signs, the Pig is the one who finds domestic bliss most often. Attentive, considerate and loyal, he will devote himself to his partner and pour a great deal of energy into his home life, striving to make it loving, close and harmonious. After all, the Pig cannot abide unpleasantness or lots of arguing. He is all for an easy and agreeable lifestyle and certainly will do nothing to disturb the equilibrium himself.

In seeking a partner the Pig should choose someone with a similarly bright and open-hearted nature, someone who is prepared to share his thoughts and interests and who also enjoys the good life. As he is prepared to give so much of himself to a relationship, when he does settle down with a partner, his life will be richer and happier as a result.

RELATIONS WITH OTHERS

Genial, sociable and sympathetic, the Pig gets on so well with others. He is certainly one of the friendliest of the Chinese signs and as a result can enjoy good relations with most of the other signs.

With a Rat

The Pig has great admiration for the Rat and with many interests in common, these two signs get on well.

In the parent–child relationship, the Rat child will respond well to the kindly and loving care of the Pig parent. There is a good understanding between them and a strong and often enduring bond. Both Pig and Rat do so value family ties.

As colleagues, the Pig and Rat recognize each other's strengths and, by joining forces, can make a successful combination. The Pig will value the Rat's resourcefulness and abilities to seek out opportunities, and provided the Rat does not take advantage of the Pig's trusting nature, between them they have the ideas, talents and abilities to go far.

In love, the Pig and Rat can find much happiness. In addition to the often strong physical attraction, they understand each other well and share many interests. They both have a fondness for the good life as well as their family life. The Pig will particularly value the supportive and attentive ways of the Rat and appreciate his charm and sense of fun. Theirs can be a successful match, with both gaining from the relationship.

With an Ox

The Pig admires the down-to-earth qualities of the Ox and with many interests in common, these two signs get on well.

In the parent–child relationship, the loving and attentive ways of the Pig parent will be a great bolster for the quiet and sometimes reserved Ox child. There will be a good understanding between them.

As colleagues, these two work well together, with their different strengths and talents proving an effective combination. The Pig will value the Ox's methodical nature and find him a resolute and dependable colleague.

In love, the Pig and Ox are well suited. They will have many interests they can share, with both having practical natures and often being fond of gardening and other outdoor pursuits. Each will value the sincerity and openness of the other, with the Pig also appreciating the quiet, caring and dependable ways of the Ox. They make a successful match.

With a Tiger

With his lively, sociable and trusting nature, the Pig has much in common with the Tiger and relations between them will be good.

In the parent–child relationship, the Pig parent will admire the Tiger child's adventurous spirit and quickness to learn, but will sometimes need to discipline him if the young Tiger is to master his restless tendencies.

As colleagues, these two like and respect each other, but they may not be the most effective combination. The Pig, while valuing the Tiger's enthusiasm and ability to come up with ideas, may feel uneasy about his more impulsive nature and inclination to take risks. With a common objective these two could accomplish much, but the Pig and Tiger generally get on better at a more social rather than business level.

In love, the Pig and Tiger make an excellent match. With strong passions and similar interests and outlooks, they are well suited. Both enjoy an active lifestyle and each will be supportive of the other. The Pig will value the Tiger's lively and positive spirit and appreciate having such a trustworthy partner. Together they can find much happiness.

With a Rabbit

The Pig has a high regard for the genial, peace-loving and sociable Rabbit and the two signs get on well.

In the parent–child relationship, there will be much love and understanding between the Pig parent and Rabbit child, with the young Rabbit responding well to the kindly and attentive ways of the Pig and doing much to please.

As colleagues, the Pig and Rabbit make a successful team. They trust and respect each other and will combine their different strengths to good effect. The Pig will particularly appreciate the Rabbit's fine organizational skills and often perceptive advice. Together these two can go far.

In love, the Pig and Rabbit are well suited. Both seek a stable, secure and harmonious existence and have a fondness for comfort and the good life. They understand each other well, with the Pig appreciating the Rabbit's judgement as well as his affectionate and good-natured ways. Theirs can be a happy and successful match.

ᐳ With a Dragon

The Pig finds the Dragon lively and interesting company and relations between the two signs are good.

In the parent–child relationship, the Pig parent will admire the Dragon child's enterprise and give him a lot of encouragement, although the young Dragon's independent-minded ways could lead to some awkward clashes. However, there is a good bond between parent and child.

As colleagues, the Pig and Dragon like and respect each other and will pool their different skills to good effect. The Pig will particularly value the Dragon's enterprising approach as well as feel reassured by having such a robust and confident colleague. Together these two can achieve a great deal.

In love, the Pig and Dragon are well suited. Both are passionate and fun-loving signs and like to live life to the full. They have many interests in common, are keen socializers and also understand each other. The Pig will value the Dragon's zest and assured manner and respect his judgement. They will each learn from their relationship and can find much happiness together.

ᐳ With a Snake

The Pig, who is so open and upfront, finds the Snake's more secretive ways a mystery. Relations between these two signs can be difficult.

In the parent–child relationship, the Pig parent may not always understand the quiet and solitary ways of a young Snake but will do much to encourage him and try to make him less reserved. The Snake child will gain much as a result as well as value the love of his well-meaning Pig parent.

As colleagues, the Pig and Snake set about their activities in different ways and agreement will be difficult. The Pig is keen on action while the Snake is given to careful planning. The Pig will be suspicious of the Snake's guarded and sometimes evasive manner. As a consequence, when working together these two do not make the most of their abilities.

In love, the Pig may for a time be intrigued by the quiet and thoughtful Snake, but with so many differences between them, the prospects are not good. The Pig enjoys an active lifestyle while the Snake prefers a more measured pace and the Pig is forthcoming while the Snake is, to the Pig, bewilderingly reserved and secretive. Theirs will be a difficult match.

With a Horse

The Pig has a high regard for the lively and enterprising Horse and relations between the two signs are good.

In the parent–child relationship, the Pig parent admires the versatility and resourcefulness of the young Horse and while he will allow his Horse child the space and time to discover his own talents, he will always be there to support and encourage. There will be much love between them.

As colleagues the Pig and Horse work well together and by combining their skills can accomplish a great deal. Both are hard and conscientious workers and the Pig will admire the Horse's enthusiasm and zest. These two make a good team.

In love, with their warm and passionate natures, the Pig and Horse are often strongly attracted to each other. Both are lively, outgoing and active. As a couple they will enjoy a good rapport, with the Pig especially valuing the Horse's sincerity and positive spirit. Theirs can be a close and successful match.

✑ With a Goat

The Pig likes the genial and easy-going ways of the Goat and the two signs get on well.

In the parent–child relationship, the Goat child will benefit from having an attentive Pig as parent and, feeling secure and loved, will often become more confident in outlook. There will be a good bond between them.

As colleagues, the Pig and Goat appreciate each other's strengths and can make a most effective combination. The Pig will recognize the Goat's more creative and innovative talents and when these are combined with his own commercial acumen, the pair could enjoy considerable success.

In love, the Goat and Pig can find much happiness. Both are passionate, appreciate the finer things in life and seek a harmonious and stress-free existence. The Pig will especially value the loving and affectionate nature of the kindly Goat. They are well suited.

✑ With a Monkey

The Pig has a great admiration for the lively and resourceful Monkey and relations between the two signs are good.

In the parent–child relationship, the Pig parent and Monkey child will share many interests, with the Pig encouraging the young Monkey and guiding him well. They enjoy a close rapport.

As colleagues, the Pig and Monkey will be quick to recognize and combine their individual talents and can make a successful team. The Pig admires the resourceful and determined style of the Monkey as well as his enterprise.

In love, the Pig and Monkey can find much happiness. Both are outgoing and sociable and yet so need a partner who cares and understands. In the Monkey, the Pig will find someone who is supportive, encouraging and such agreeable company. With many mutual interests and an active social life, there will be a lot of fun in their relationship and they make an excellent match.

With a Rooster

The Pig finds the Rooster interesting company and the two signs get on well.

In the parent–child relationship, the Pig parent will applaud the inquisitive nature of the Rooster child and do much to support him. The young Rooster will learn much from his parent and there will be a good understanding between them.

As colleagues, both work hard and are honourable in their business dealings. However, while the Pig will think highly of the Rooster's efficient and orderly ways, he could sometimes find his more exacting nature an inhibiting influence, especially as the Pig is so geared up for action.

In love, the Pig and Rooster can both gain from their relationship, with the Pig often becoming more methodical and organized as a result of the Rooster's influence. As both value their domestic and social life and are keen on the outdoors, there is much they can enjoy together. However, for the relationship to endure, they will need to be understanding of each other. The Pig may wish the Rooster was sometimes less candid. With care they can, though, form a fine and meaningful relationship.

With a Dog

The Pig has a great admiration for the loyal and trustworthy Dog and, with much in common, the two signs get on well.

In the parent–child relationship, the genial Pig parent can do much to help dispel some of the young Dog's worrying tendencies as well as help him to become more confident in outlook. There is a great bond between parent and child.

As colleagues the Pig and Dog have a great respect for each other's skills and, by combining these, can do well together. Both are open and honourable in their dealings, with the Pig respecting the Dog's judgement and views.

In love, the Pig and Dog are well suited. They are understanding and supportive of each other and, with their many mutual interests, will have much in common. Both strive for a settled and stable home life, and the Pig will particularly value having such a loyal and dependable partner. Theirs can be a successful and meaningful match.

✎ With another Pig

The Pig can enjoy a marvellous rapport with another of his sign. Relations between two Pigs will often be excellent.

In the parent–child relationship, there will be much love between a Pig parent and Pig child. The Pig child will feel content in a loving and easy-going Pig household, although the parent will need to guide, encourage and sometimes discipline the young Pig in order to make him use his talents wisely. However, there will be a good bond between them.

As colleagues, two Pigs will be an inspiration to each other. Both are hard-working and are often astute in business and commercial dealings. With their sound judgement and talents they have the makings of an excellent team.

In love, two Pigs can find much happiness together. With similar interests and outlooks they enjoy a close rapport and each will be supportive of the other. They know how to enjoy themselves but at the same time will value a settled and harmonious existence. They are well suited.

SUCCESS AND LIFE

Keen, eager and game, the Pig enjoys so many of the experiences and opportunities that life offers. True, there will be some mistakes as well as some difficult lessons to be learnt, but the Pig is robust and invariably comes out smiling.

His childhood years will often be a happy time. Well-behaved and generally content, the young Pig will find it easy to get on with others and will be popular. However, without a certain degree of guidance and discipline he could sometimes be tempted to put play before his schoolwork and this could suffer if he is not careful.

On completing his education the Pig is not likely to have given much thought to what he really wants to do. The Pig tends not to be a long-term planner and as a consequence could spend his early adult years frequently changing his job or investigating a variety of career possibilities. As Henry Ford, a Pig, so wisely said, 'Failure is the opportunity to begin again more intelligently.' In his early working life the Pig could make several starts, each time discovering more about himself and widening his experience.

However, while the Pig's early working life may be uncertain, his personal life is likely to be active and pleasurable, with a great deal of socializing and enjoying the passions of love. This can be a happy time for the Pig, but difficulties – and disasters – could also lurk. Should his work or a relationship run into sudden difficulty, it can affect the Pig deeply. Unless he is well supported, he does run the risk of a period of decline and despondency. However, it is often during such a time that the Pig will come to realize that it is *he* who is master of his destiny and will resolve to get his life back on course. For many Pigs the seeds of success are sown during more troubled times. And once the Pig has reason *and* the motivation to better himself, he really will display his incredible power and energy and strive to achieve his goals.

In his early adult years the Pig's fortunes can fluctuate, but once he has decided upon the right type of work for him and enjoys the love of another, then he will be on course for a much more settled and happy existence. Being so caring as well as fond of comfort and high standards, he will work hard, often earn a good living and be very supportive towards his loved ones.

The Pig's maturer years can be a satisfying time and when he retires, he will certainly savour the fruits of his labours, pursuing his varied interests and enjoying the love and friendship of many.

Like us all, the Pig will make mistakes and have his struggles, but his capacity to give, to love and to make a difference make him a survivor – and an ultimate winner.

FAMOUS PIGS

Bryan Adams, Woody Allen, Julie Andrews, Fred Astaire, Humphrey Bogart, James Cagney, Maria Callas, Richard Chamberlain, Hillary Rodham Clinton, Glenn Close, Sir Noël Coward, Oliver Cromwell, Billy Crystal, the Dalai Lama, Richard Dreyfuss, Sheena Easton, Ben Elton, Ralph Waldo Emerson, Henry Ford, Emmylou Harris, William Randolph Hearst, Ernest Hemingway, Henry VIII, Alfred Hitchcock, Sir Elton John, Tommy Lee Jones, Carl Gustav Jung, Boris Karloff, Stephen King, Nastassja Kinski, Kevin Kline, Hugh Laurie, David Letterman, Jerry Lee Lewis, Marcel Marceau, Ricky Martin, Johnny Mathis, Meat Loaf, Wolfgang Amadeus Mozart, Camilla Parker Bowles, Michael Parkinson, Luciano Pavarotti, Prince

Rainier of Monaco, Maurice Ravel, Ronald Reagan, Françoise
Sagan, Pete Sampras, Carlos Santana, Arnold Schwarzenegger,
Steven Spielberg, Tracey Ullman, Jules Verne, Michael Winner,
the Duchess of York.

SUCCESS TIPS FOR THE PIG

The Pig has many great abilities. He is kindly, well-meaning and
is prepared to work hard. However, he does not always make as
much of himself as he could. He would do better to give more
thought to the longer term. In his work he should consider skills
and qualifications that would be useful for him and work to
obtain them and, in his personal life and his interests, he could
find that by setting himself projects and objectives, he is able to
make better use of his time. Whether career aspirations, home
and personal projects or even travel plans, whatever his objectives, by thinking ahead and setting himself goals, the Pig will be
better focused and able to achieve more as a result.

In some instances the Pig also lacks a certain sophistication.
He may mean well and be determined, but he can lose out to
the more competitive and assertive. Although the Pig is not one
to readily change his nature or style, believing his qualities are
what count, on some occasions it is worth him making that extra
effort. It need not be much, but a little more push, better presentation and a greater determination can make *all* the difference,
especially when being interviewed or looking to advance. The
Pig has what it takes to get on, but he needs to take more care
when putting himself across in competitive situations.

Financially, the Pig may have considerable earning ability
and possess good judgement, but he can be indulgent and
spend freely. Although he does enjoy the fruits of his labours, he
could find it in his interests to conserve his resources and per-

haps think twice when tempted by an impulsive purchase. By planning his purchases and saving towards specific items, such as a really good holiday or new equipment for his home, he could find he makes better use of his money and acquires something which will generally mean more to him.

The Pig has a great appetite for life and throws his energies into it. He gives his all, but as he drives himself so hard, he does need to look after himself. The Pig should make sure he keeps himself in good form and if he is sedentary for much of the day, he should make up for this by taking suitable exercise. Similarly, with his fondness for food (and drink), he may need to watch his weight. To be at his best, the Pig does need to give more thought to his well-being. He could find regular exercise of great benefit and in some cases fun to do as well.

SOME FINAL THOUGHTS FROM PIGS

Life is a series of experiences, each one of which makes us bigger, even though sometimes it is hard to realize this.
Henry Ford

Nothing is particularly hard if you divide it into small jobs.
Henry Ford

If there is any great secret of success in life, it lies in the ability to put yourself in the other person's place and to see things from his point of view – as well as your own.
Henry Ford

Enthusiasm is the yeast that makes your hopes rise to the stars.
Enthusiasm is the sparkle in your eyes, the swing in your gait,
the grip of your hand, the irresistible surge of will and energy to
execute your ideas.
Henry Ford

Sow a thought and you reap an act;
Sow an act and you reap a habit;
Sow a habit and you reap a character;
Sow a character and you reap a destiny.
Ralph Waldo Emerson

All life is an experiment. The more experiments you make, the
better.
Ralph Waldo Emerson

Be not the slave of your own past – plunge into the sublime seas,
dive deep, and swim far, so you shall come back with self-
respect, with new power, with an advanced experience, that
shall explain and overlook the old.
Ralph Waldo Emerson

For the resolute and determined there is time and opportunity.
Ralph Waldo Emerson

To laugh often and much, to win the respect of intelligent people
and the affection of children, to earn the appreciation of honest
critics and endure the betrayal of false friends, to appreciate
beauty, to find the best in others, to leave the world a bit better,
whether by a healthy child, a garden patch, or a redeemed social
condition, to know even one life has breathed easier because
you lived, this is to have succeeded.
Ralph Waldo Emerson

A Final Thought

This book opened with the words of Lao-tzu: 'Knowing others is wisdom, knowing yourself is enlightenment.' Knowing yourself is so necessary to get on in life. I hope that having discovered more about your Chinese sign, you can use this information to your advantage.

You are the master of your own destiny. Use your strengths well. They are the keys to your destiny and your success in life. Once you know yourself and take action to realize your dreams, you can unlock the doors to your own potential.

Good luck.

And may the success you want in life one day be yours.